THE INTERACTIVE

by Sidney Harris

Crisp Publications
Menlo Park

THE INTERACTIVE TOASTER

Sidney Harris

CREDITS
Managing Editor: **Kathleen Barcos**
Editor: **Phil Gerould**
Designer: **ExecuStaff**
Typesetting: **ExecuStaff**
Cover Design: **Sidney Harris**

The cartoons in this book have been previously published by the following publications: Barron's, Chicago Magazine, Datamation, Harvard Business Review Hemispheres, Management Review, Playboy, The New Yorker, The Wall Street Journal, the late Punch and a few other extinct periodicals.

Of the 118 drawings in this collection, 10 appeared originally in The New Yorker and were copyrighted © in the years 1981, 1982, 1983, 1985, 1988 and 1995.

Distribution to the U.S. Trade:

National Book Network, Inc.
4720 Boston Way
Lanham, MD 20706
1-800-462-6420

Library of Congress Catalog Card Number 96-85525
Harris, Sidney
The Interactive Toaster
ISBN 1-56052-408-1

This book is printed on recyclable paper with soy ink.

Introduction

The keen perspective of Sidney Harris's jabs to the soft underbelly of business has rattled and amused readers of *The New Yorker, The Wall Street Journal, Science* and other leading publications for over three decades. This collection demonstrates the freshness of his eye and the sharpness of his wit in everything from the joys of the interactive toaster to the pain of the power hot dog. If there is now a way to look at cartoons about the travails of everyday business life, it is because Sidney Harris put us on that path and kept us there.

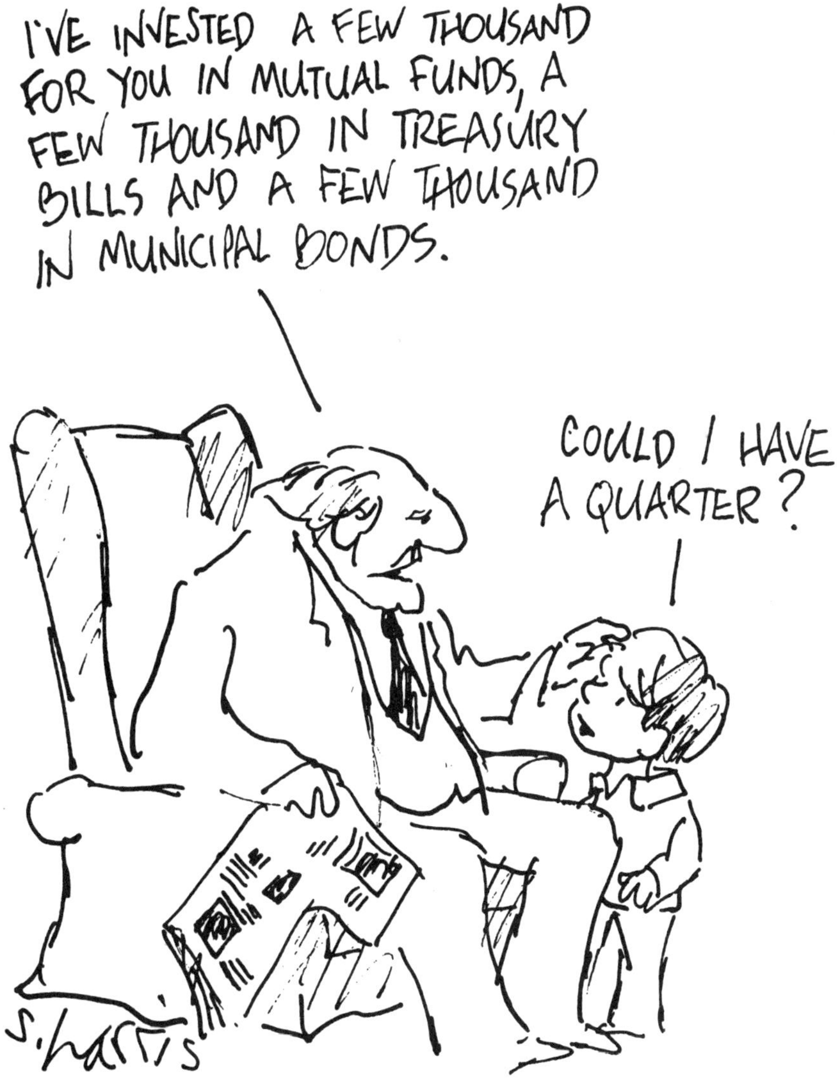
I'VE INVESTED A FEW THOUSAND FOR YOU IN MUTUAL FUNDS, A FEW THOUSAND IN TREASURY BILLS AND A FEW THOUSAND IN MUNICIPAL BONDS.
COULD I HAVE A QUARTER?
S. Harris

ATTEMPTING TO UNDERSTAND THE MARKET:
MERRILL LYNCH, PIERCE, FENNER & FREUD

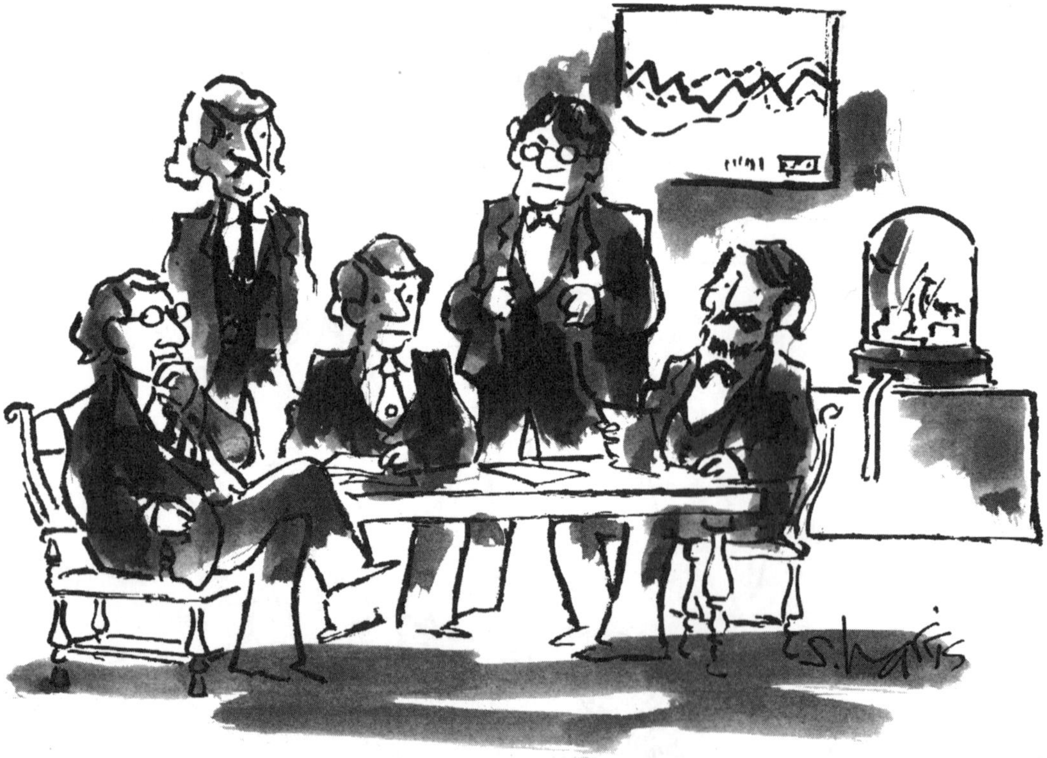
S. Harris

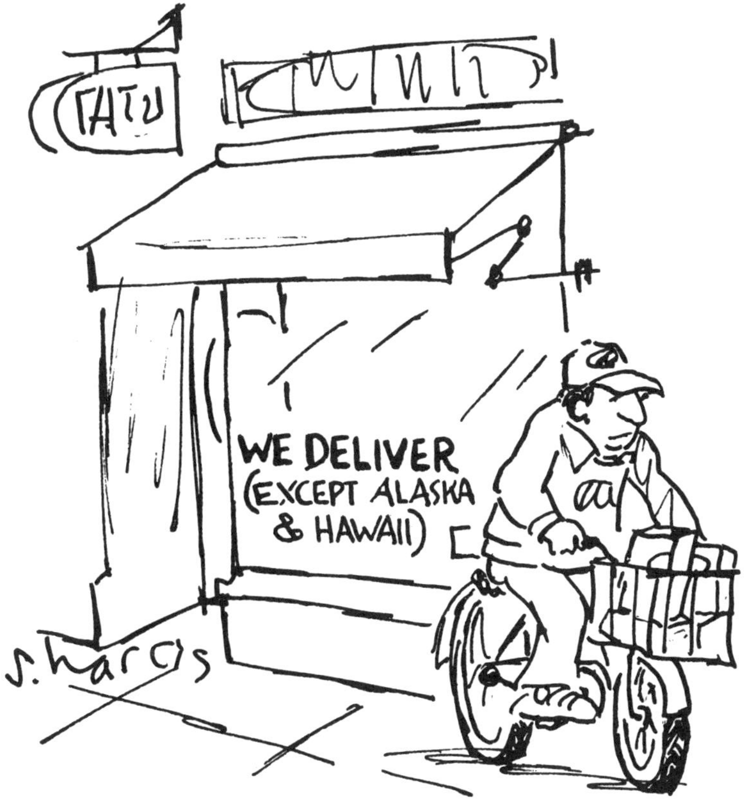
WE DELIVER
(EXCEPT ALASKA
& HAWAII)
S. Harris

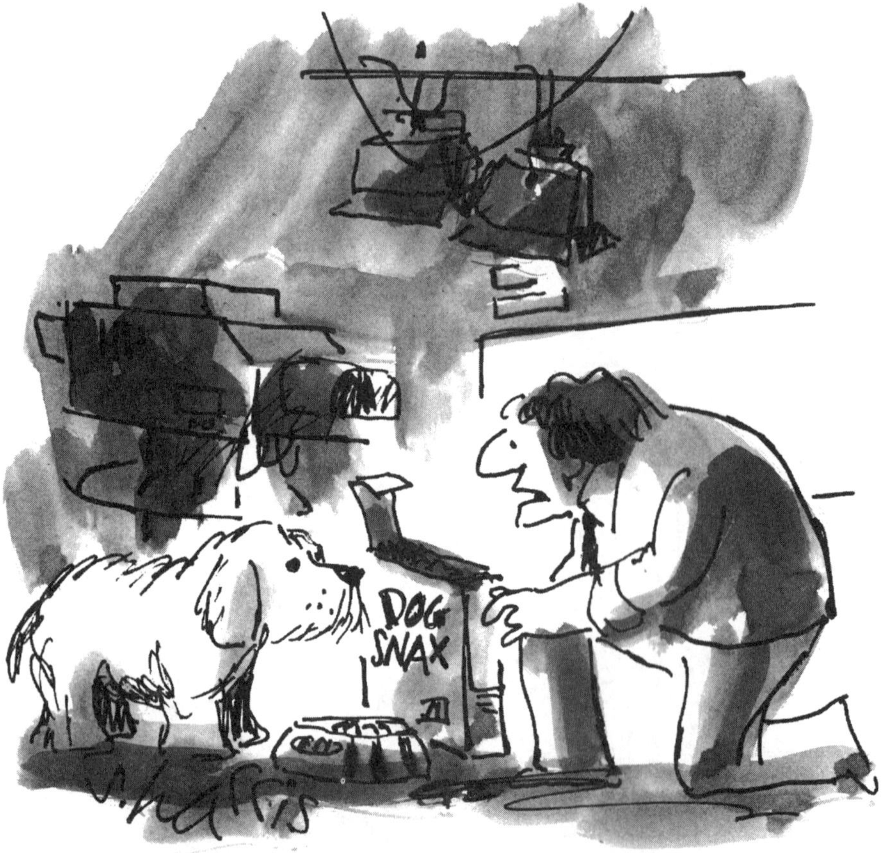
DOG
SNAX

"The F.C.C. says we have to document our claims, so here's what I want you to do . . ."

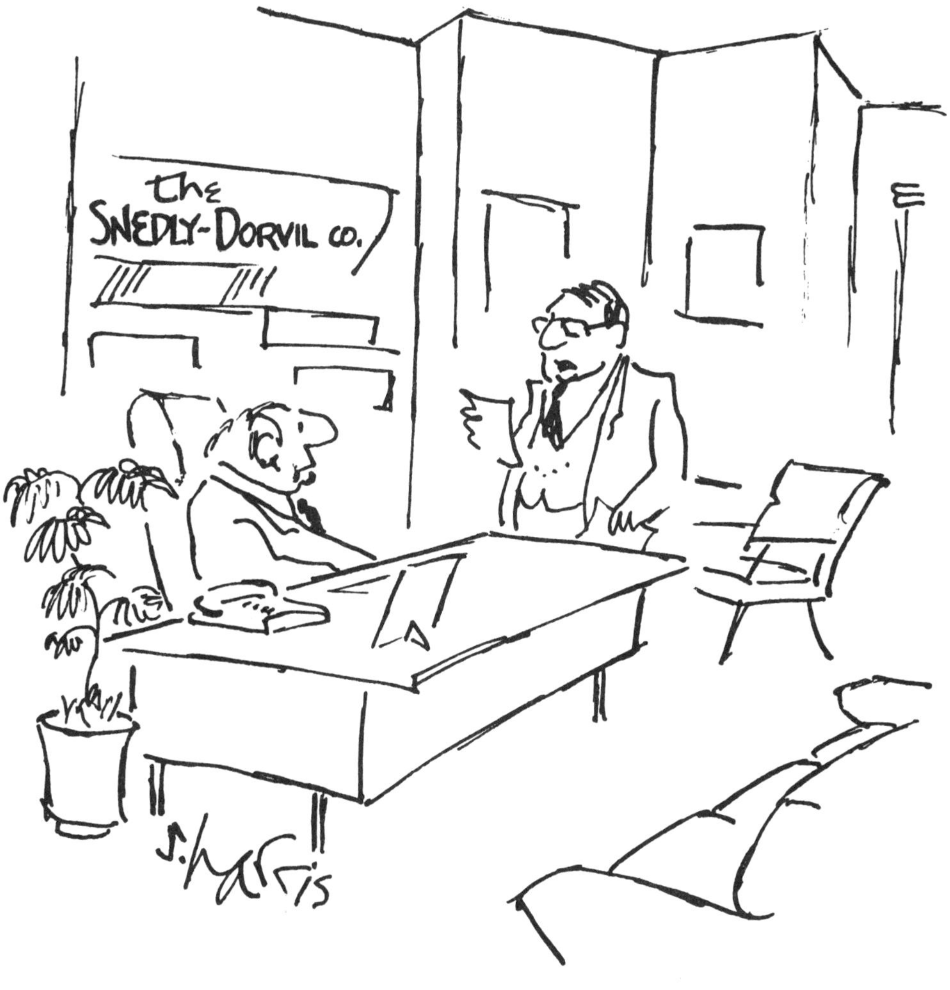
the
SNEDLY-DORVIL CO.
S. Harris

"The Dorvil people feel that the merger was a mistake. They want out, they want half the company's assets and they want child support."

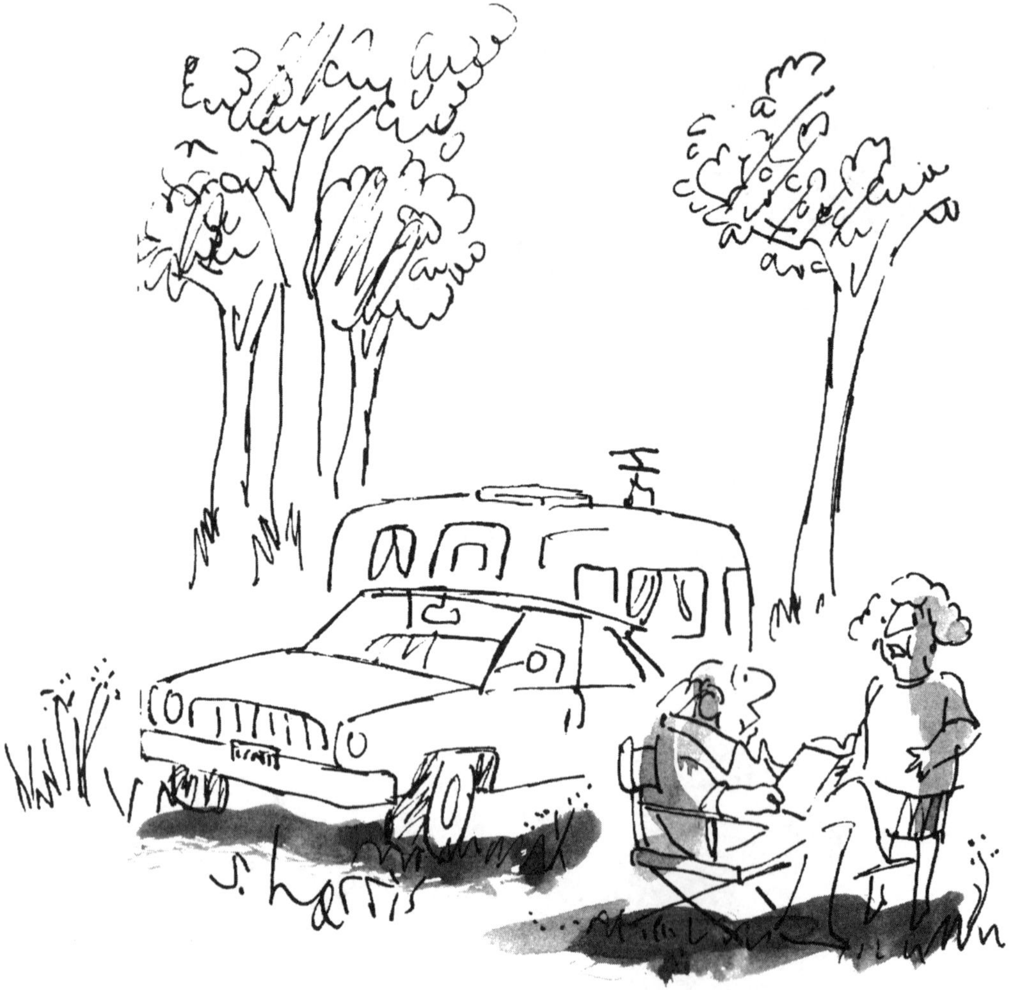
s. harris

"You call this a golden parachute?"

"*I was just beginning to* think *about my portfolio.*
Now you're telling me to re-think *it.*"

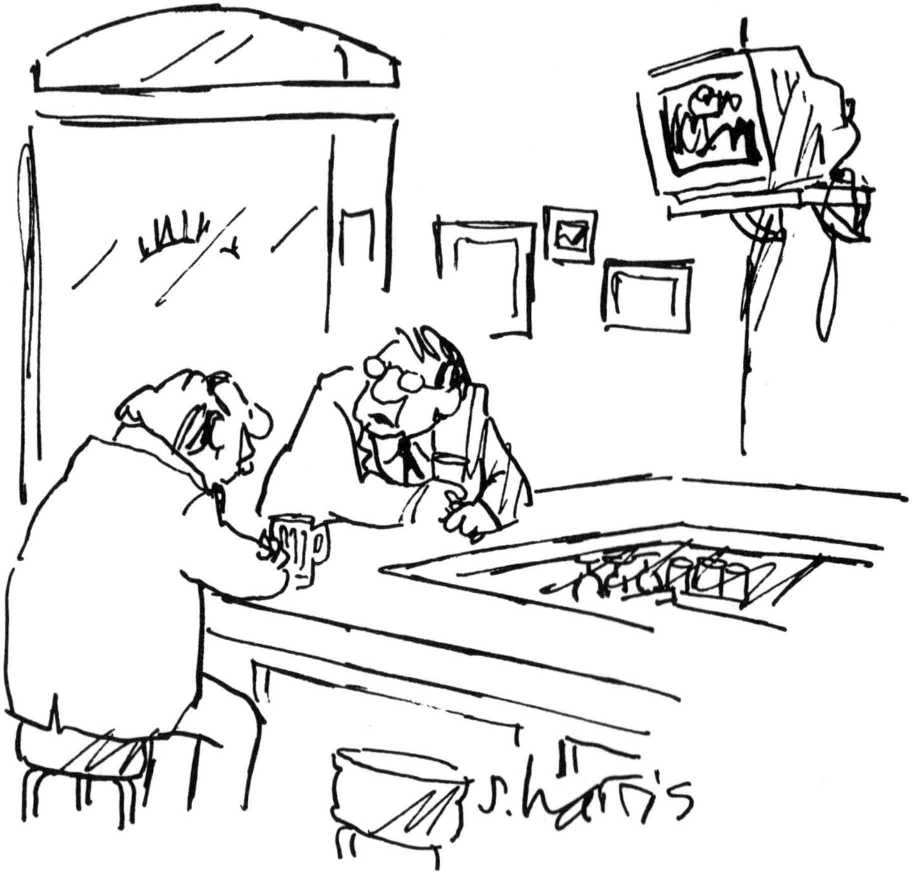
S. harris

"I thought I was pre-med. Turned out I was really pre-real estate."

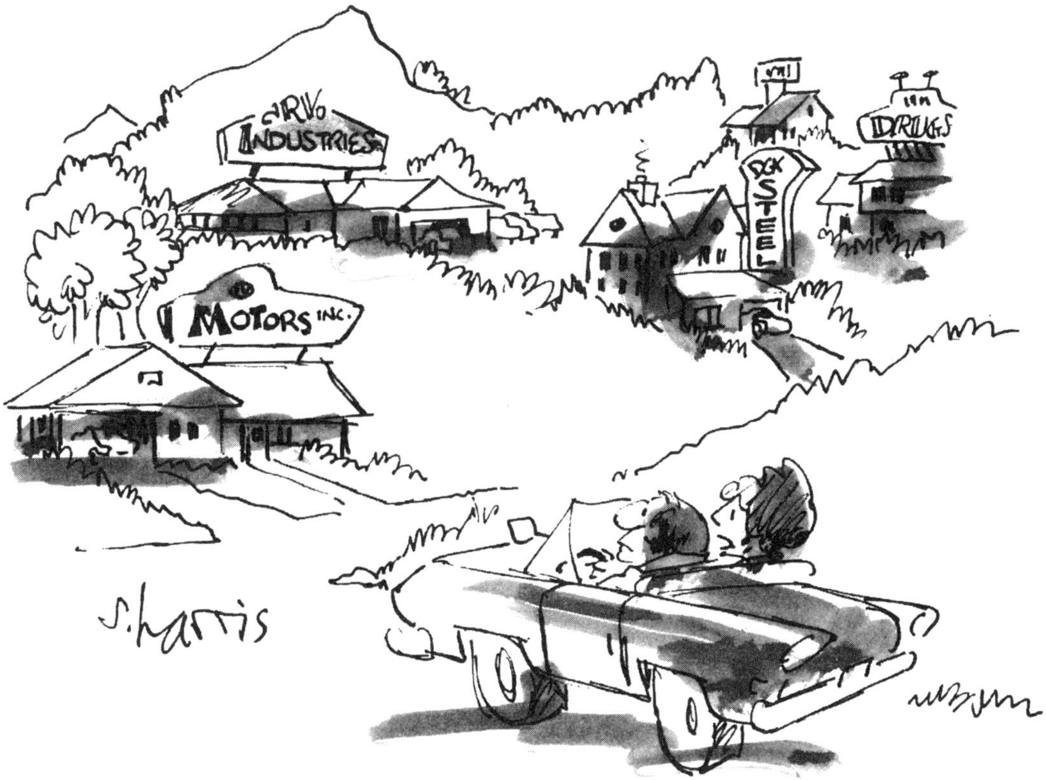
INDUSTRIES
MOTORS INC.
STEEL
DRUGS
S. Harris

"It appears that more and more people are working at home these days."

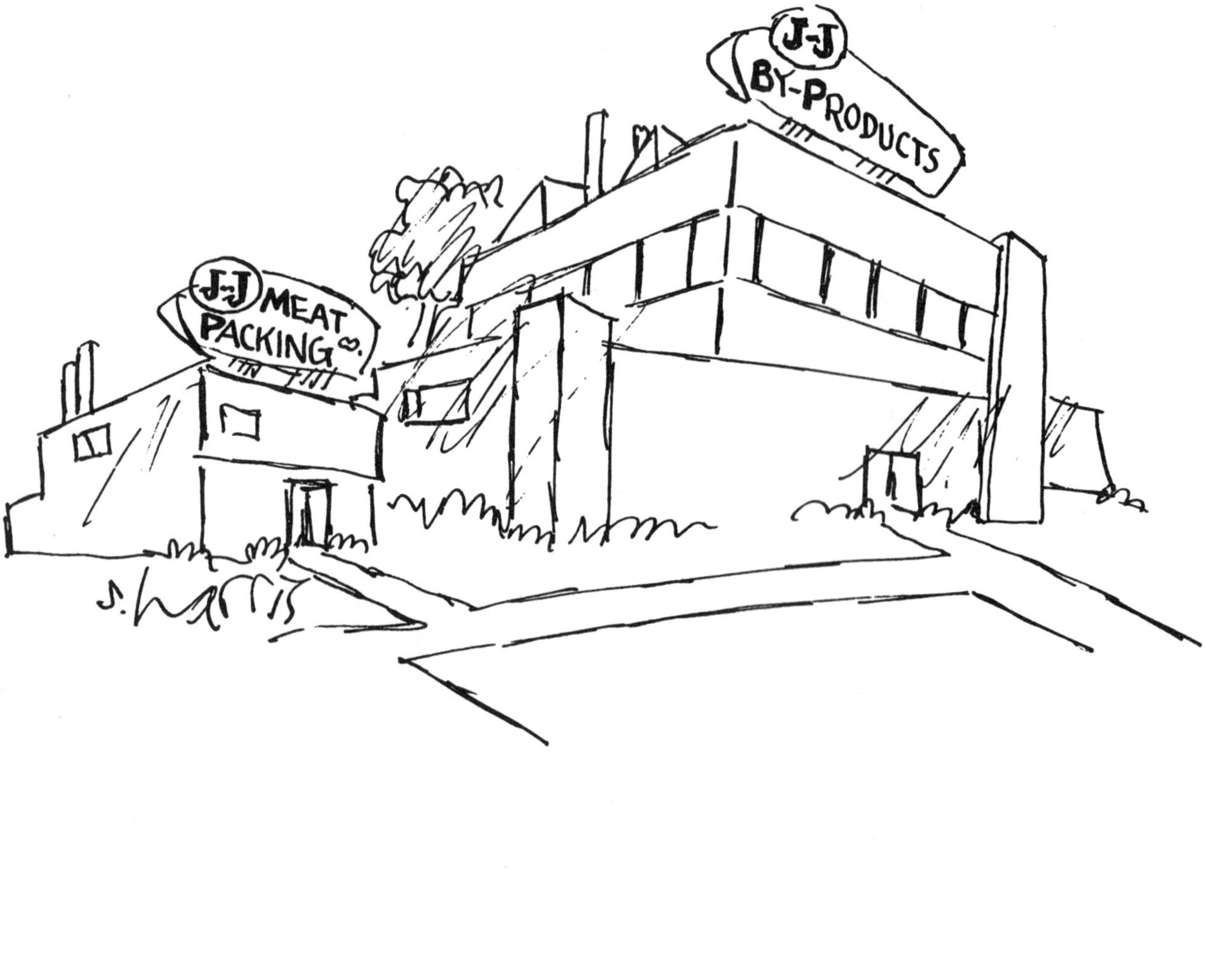
J-J BY-PRODUCTS
J-J MEAT PACKING CO.
S. Harris

"*These kids from the business schools—
they know that gold is where it's at.*"

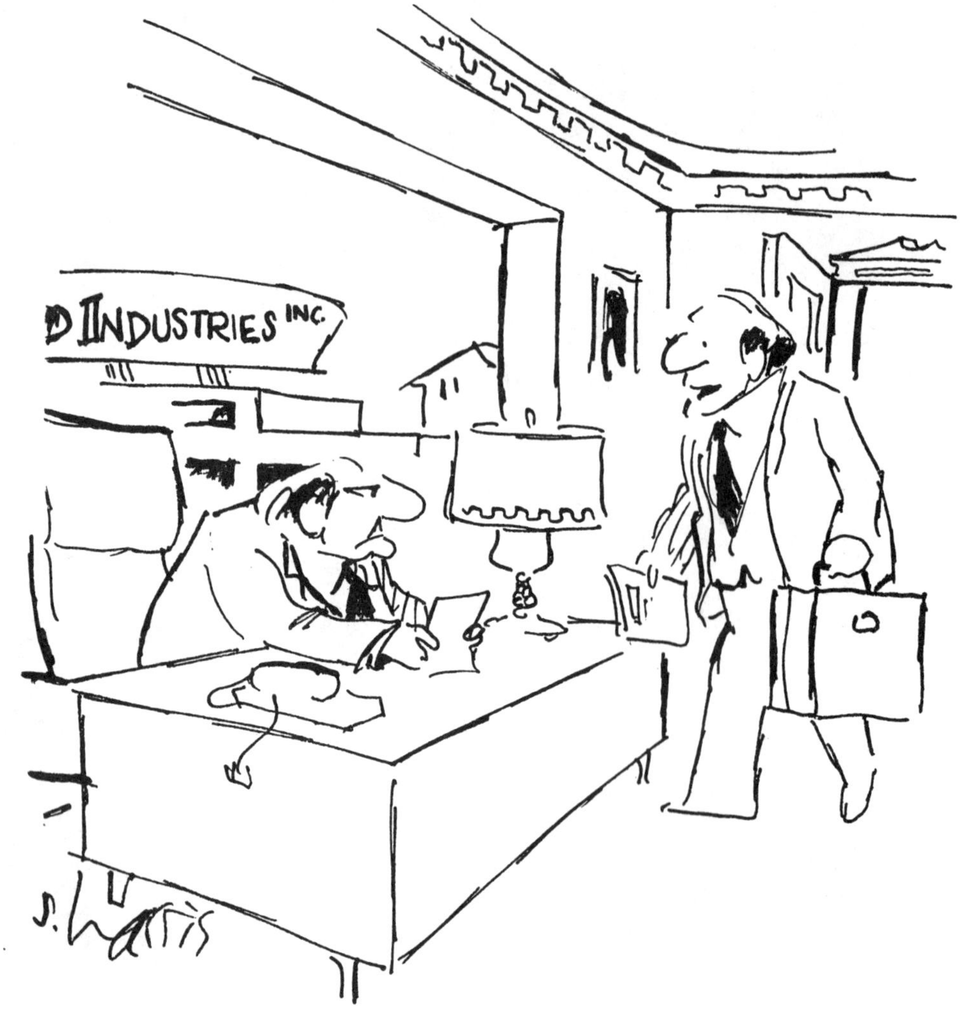
INDUSTRIES INC.

"I'm afraid I lied to your receptionist, sir. I'm not here to discuss the Amalgamated merger. I'm here to sell you some brushes."

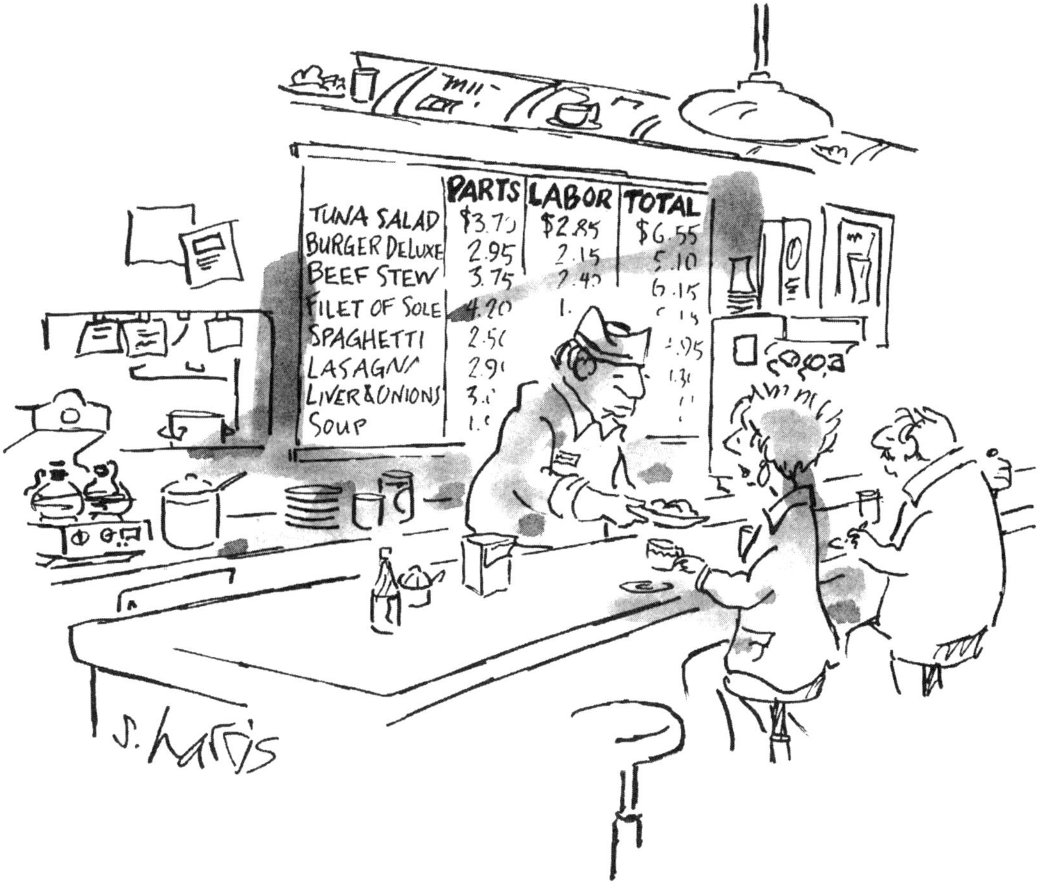
PARTS LABOR TOTAL
TUNA SALAD $2.85 $6.55
BURGER DELUXE 2.95 5.10
BEEF STEW 6.15
FILET OF SOLE
SPAGHETTI
LIVER & ONIONS
SOUP
S. Harris

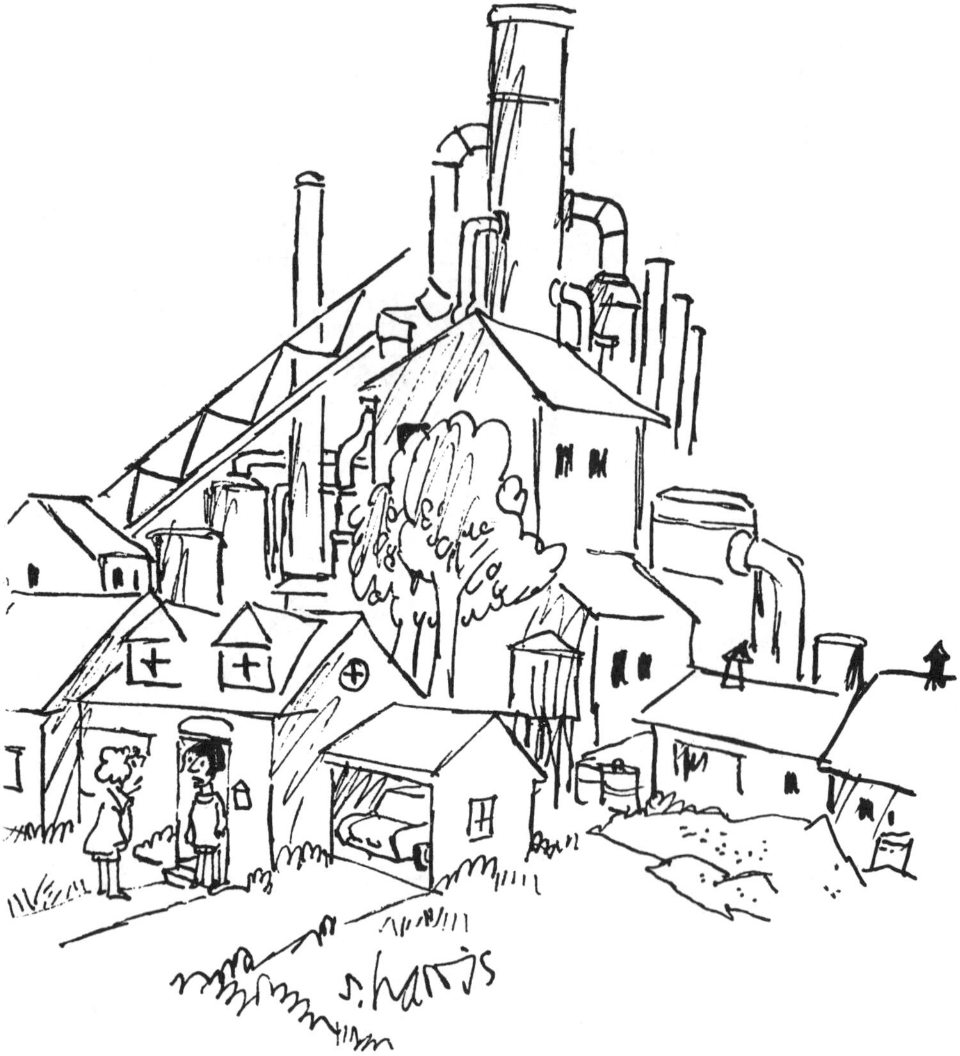
s. harris

"Yes, the business has become bigger, but Fred still likes to work at home."

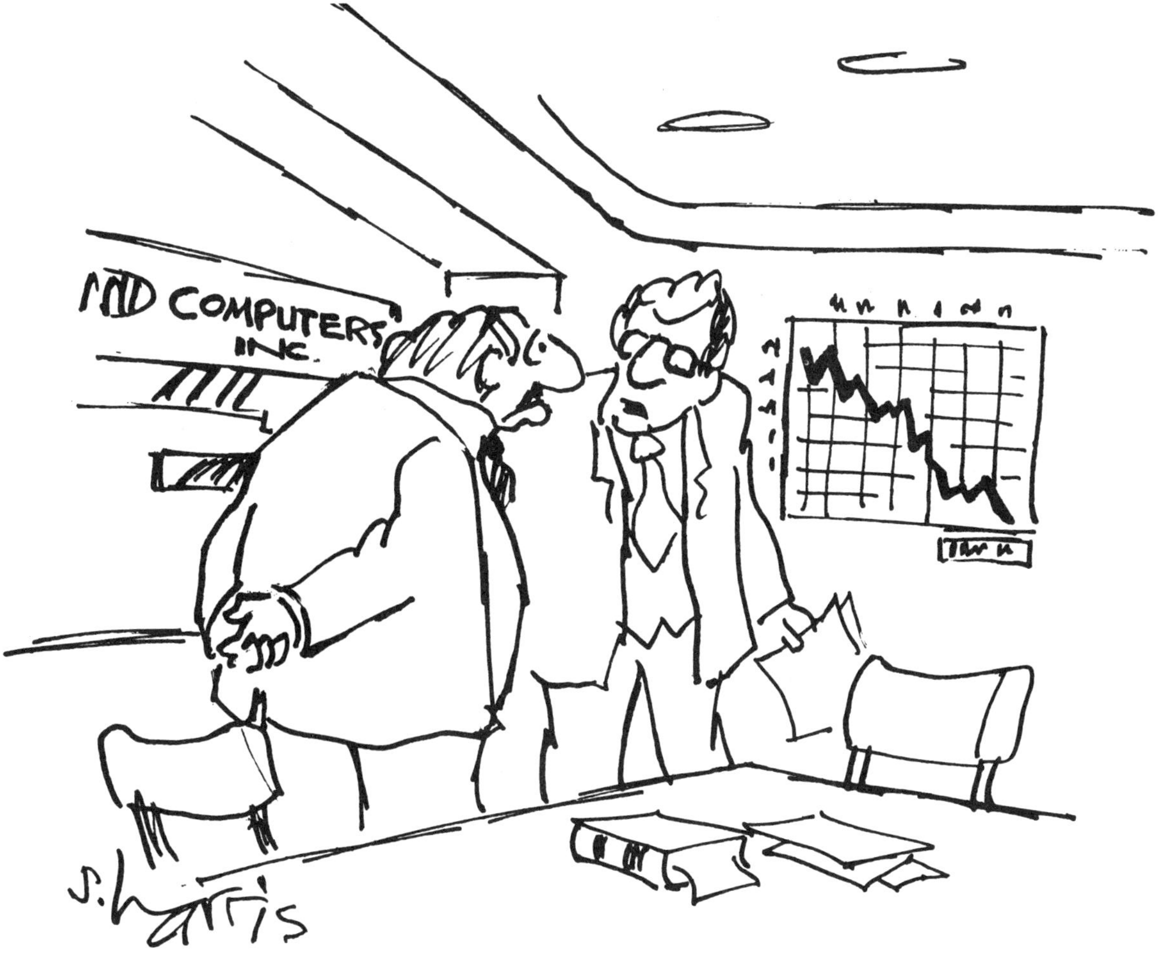
COMPUTERS
INC

"What it comes down to is our software is too hard and our hardware is too soft."

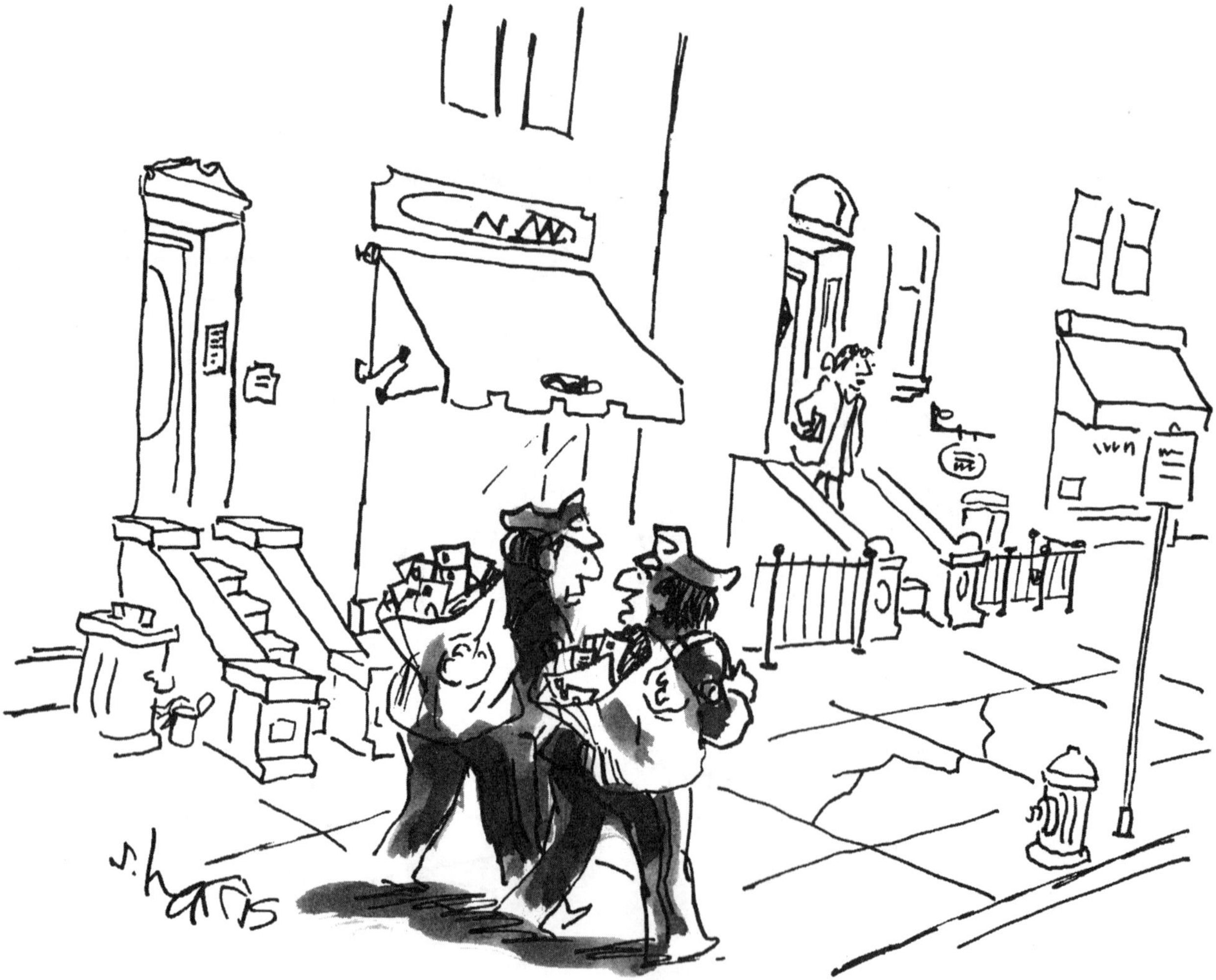
s.harris

"Once the neighborhood really gets into e-mail and voice mail, we'll be out of here."

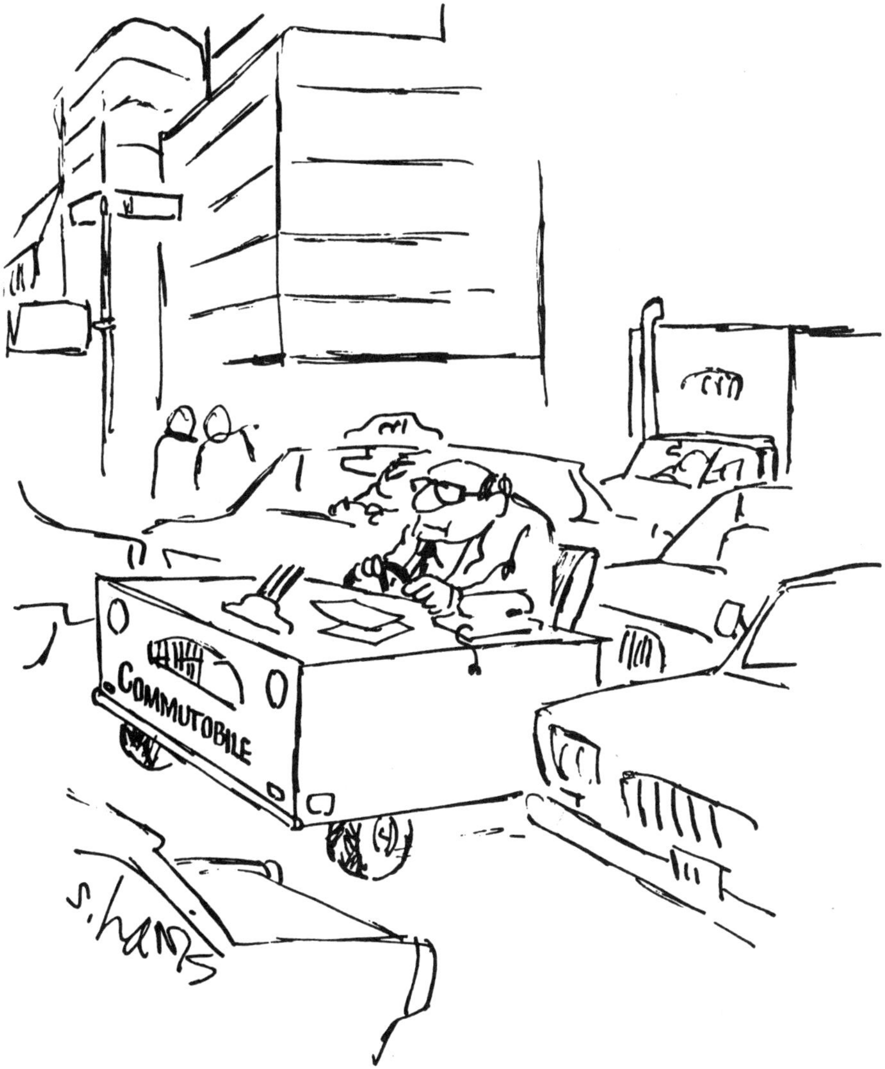
COMMUTOBILE
S. HARRIS

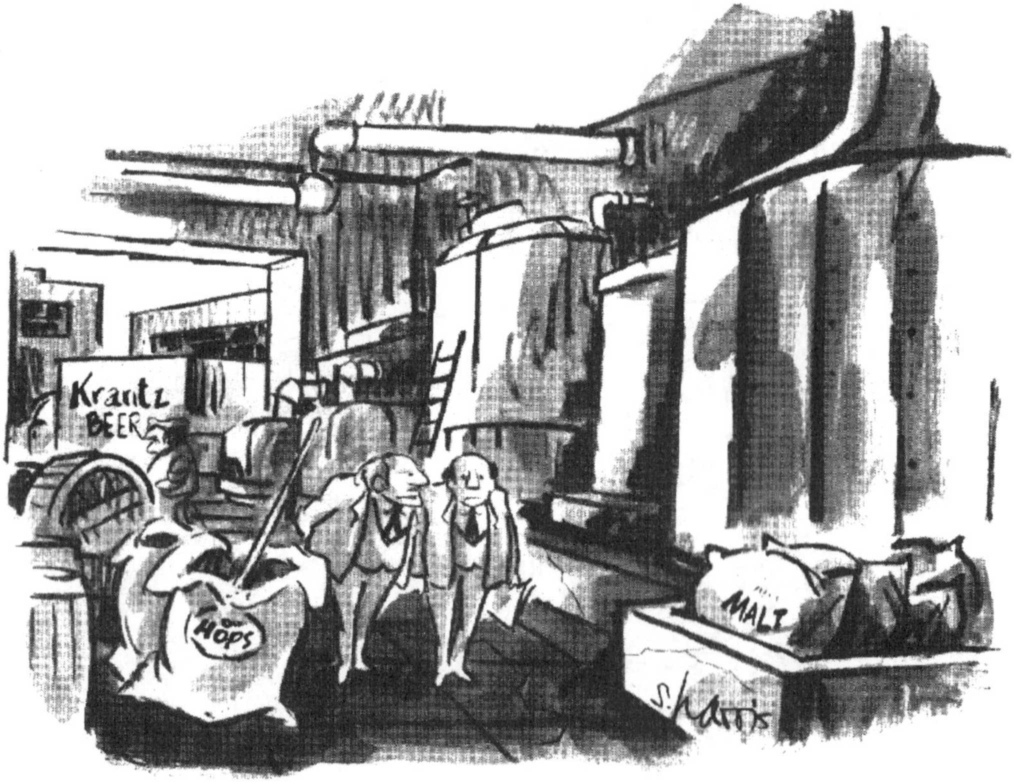
Krantz
BEER
HOPS
MALT
S. Harris

"But our secret ingredient is large quantities of Hilberg beer."

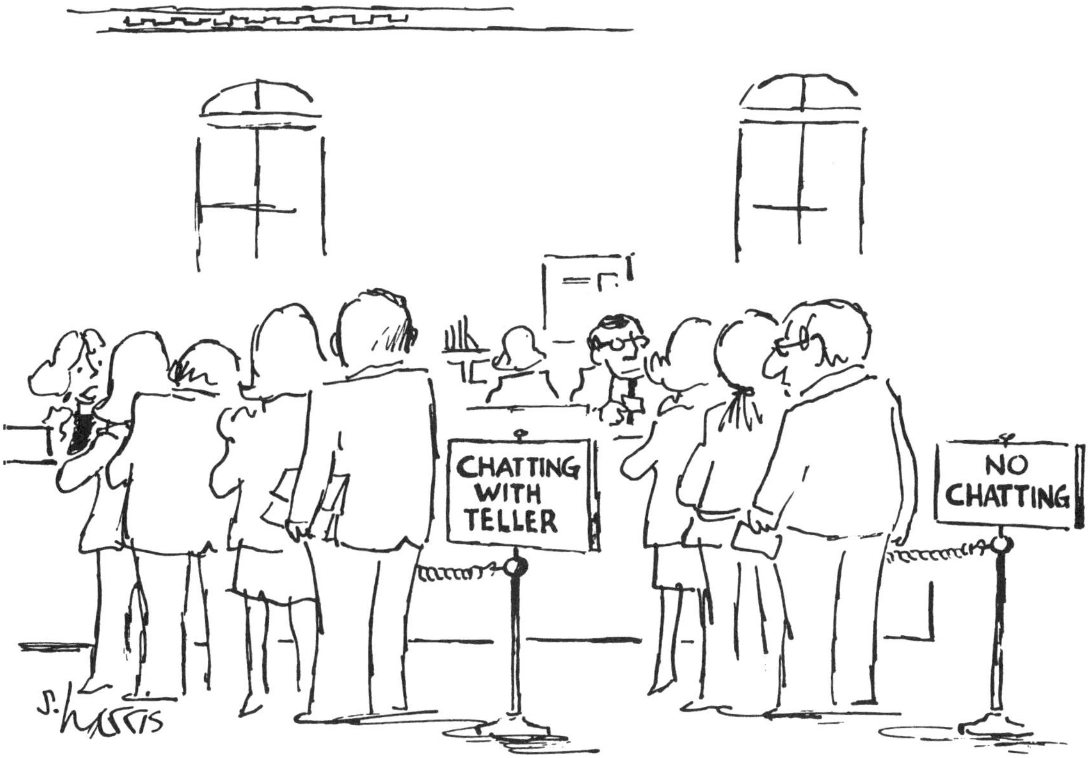
CHATTING WITH TELLER
NO CHATTING

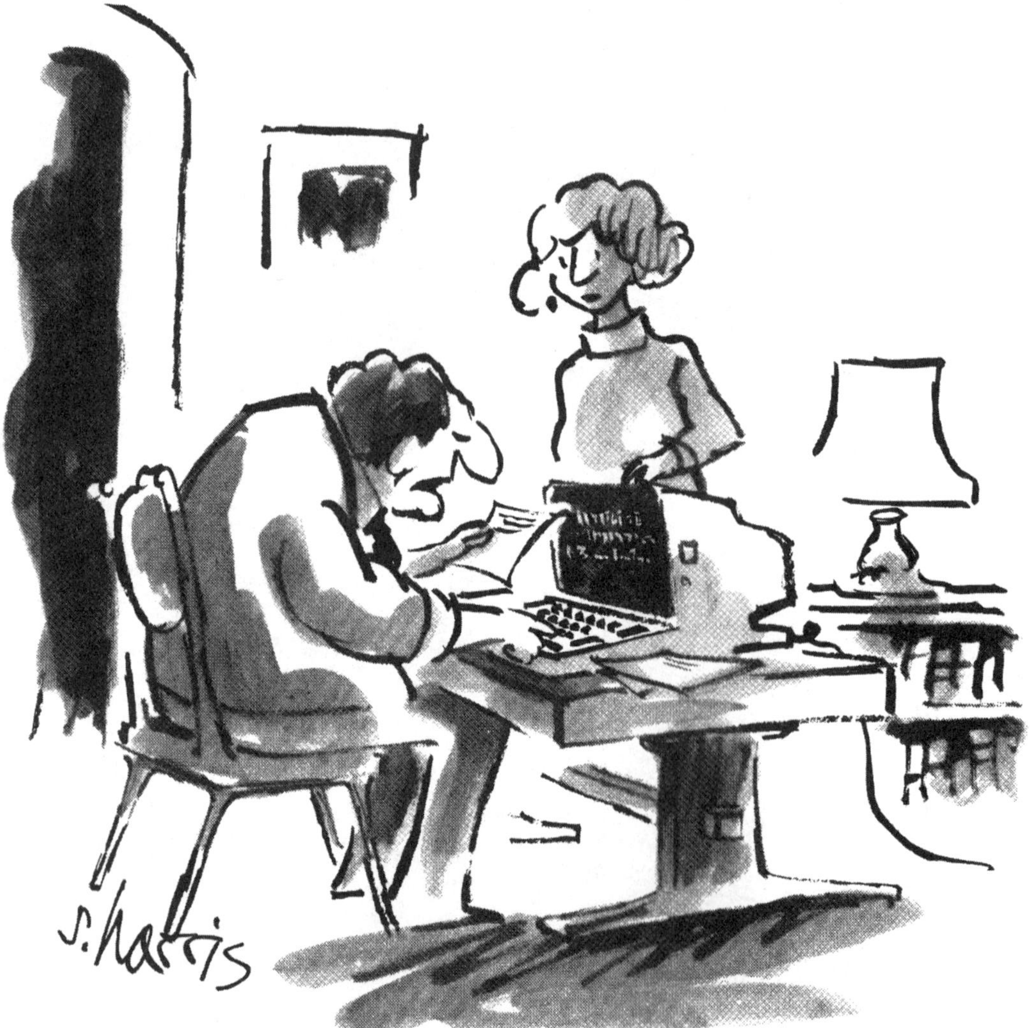
s.harris

*"It's **not** a game called 'Illegally Transferring Funds.' It's what I'm **doing** . . . illegallly transferring funds."*

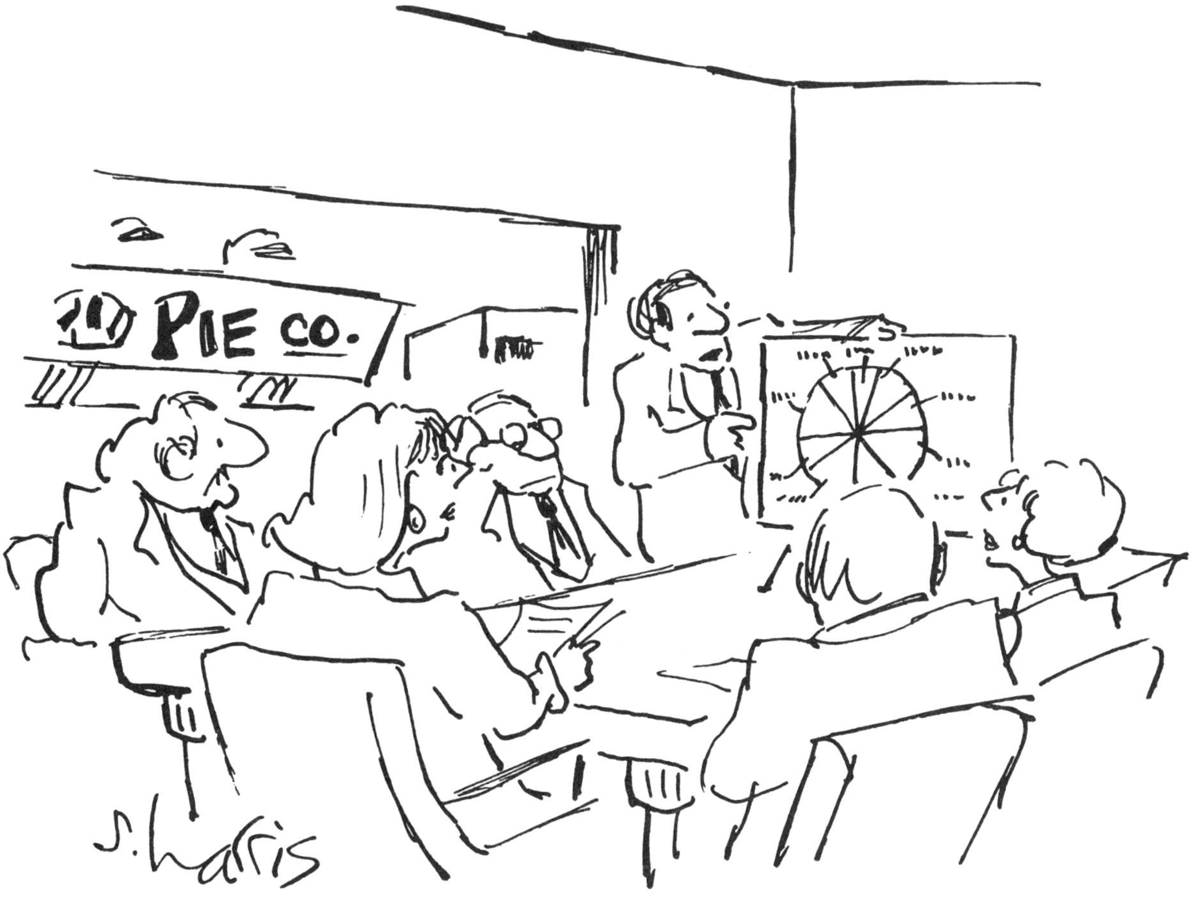
PIE CO.
S. Harris

"Each slice of the pie represents slices of pie."

"We've gone over your budget very carefully, Mr. Thorne.
Unfortunately the network does not sell 7-second spots."

SEE DISTRICT DIRECTORS
Refer to Supervisors
APPLY TO ASSISTANT MANAGERS
INQUIRE OF CLERKS
MEMBERS OF BUREAUCRACY DEMAND HIGHER WAGES
S. Harris

A DAY IN THE KITCHEN

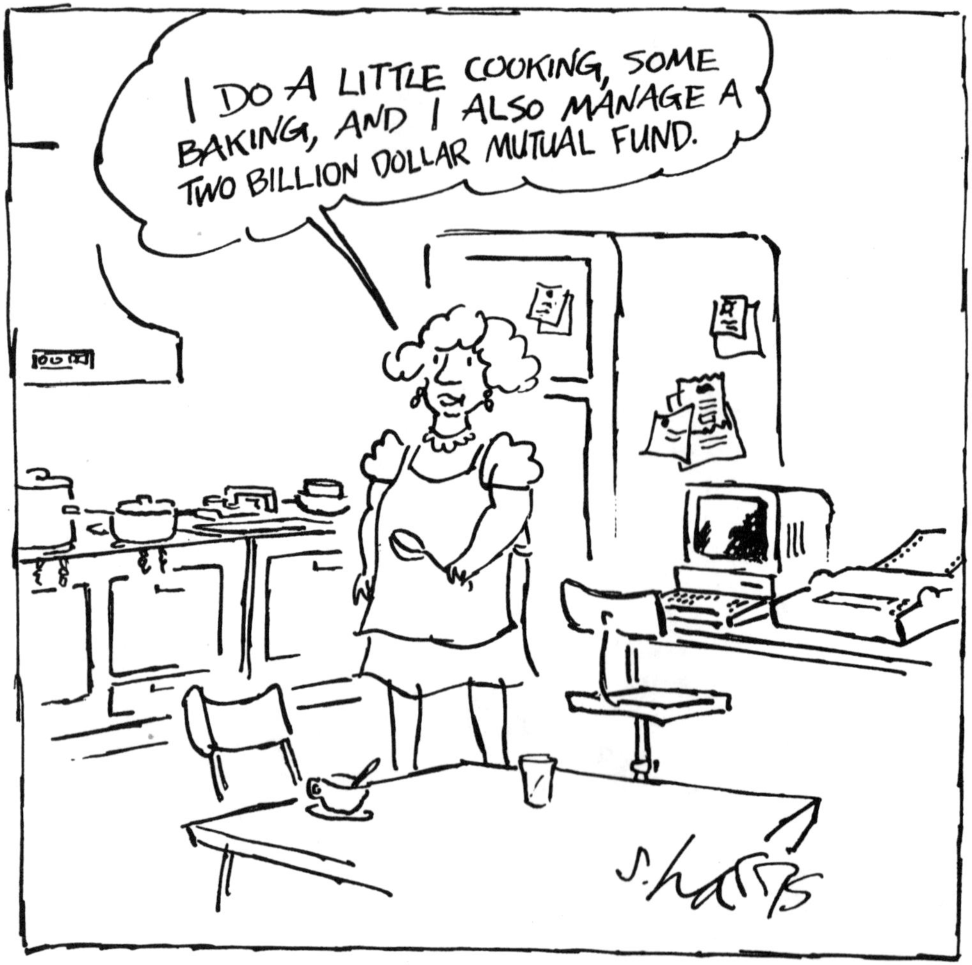
I DO A LITTLE COOKING, SOME BAKING, AND I ALSO MANAGE A TWO BILLION DOLLAR MUTUAL FUND.

THE MANIA CONTINUES...
You all know the Albright family down the road... we're merging with them.
S. Harris

I must find out how to control the rights when it comes out on parchment.
S. Harris

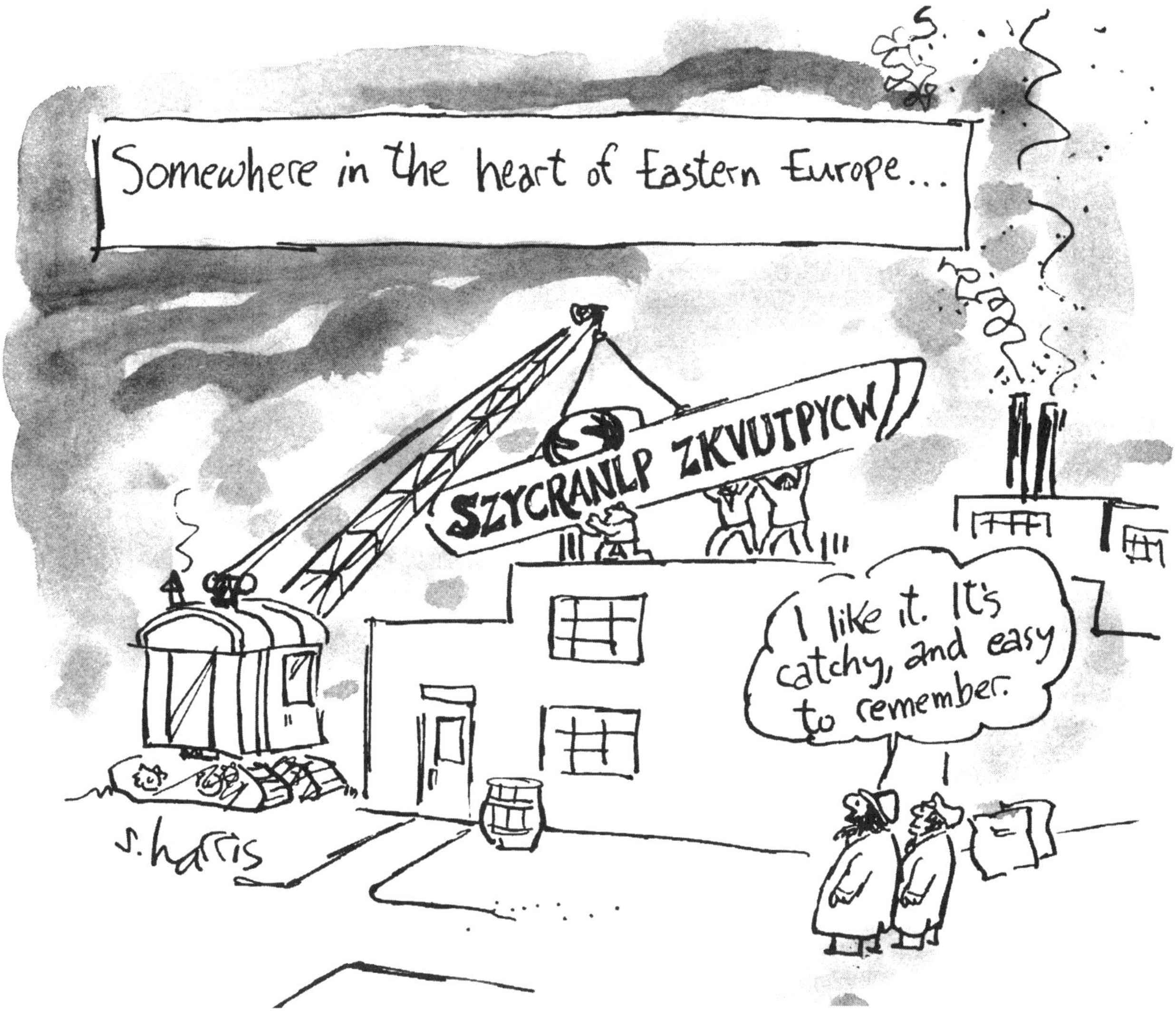
Somewhere in the heart of Eastern Europe...
SZYCRANLP ZKVUTPYCW
I like it. It's catchy, and easy to remember.
S. harris

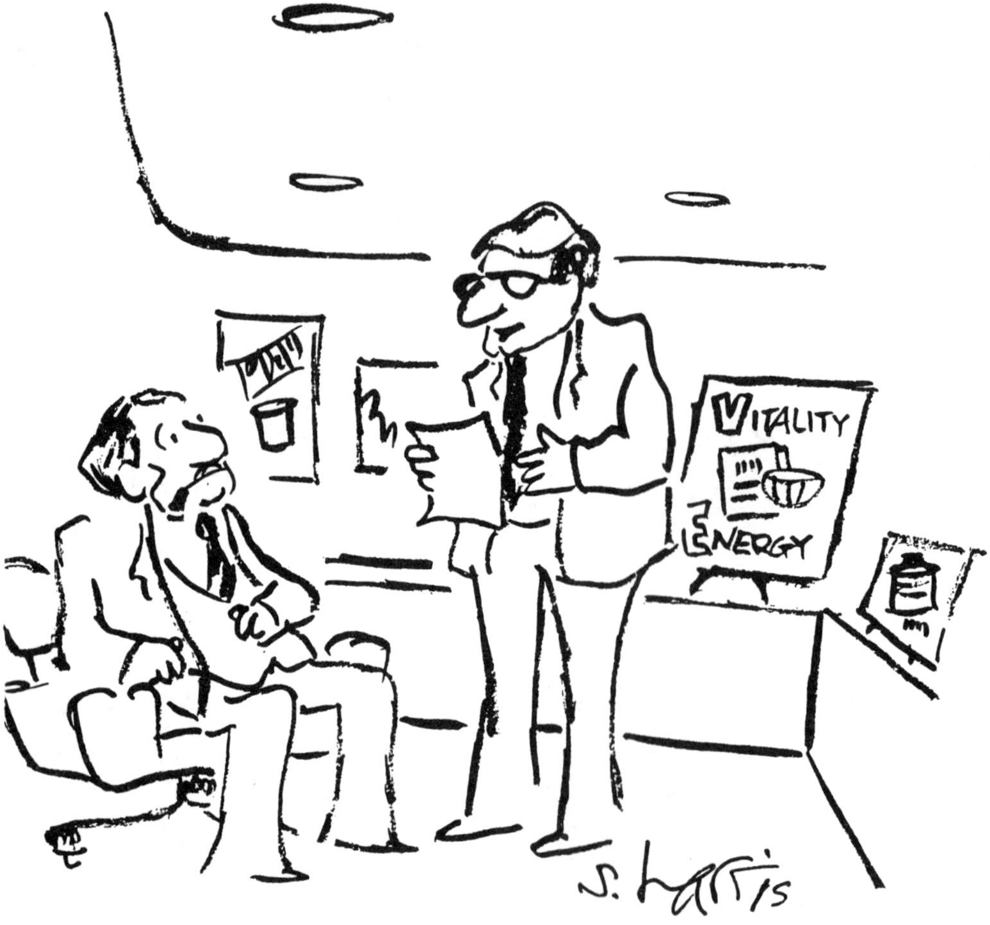
VITALITY
ENERGY
S. Harris

"They want us to back up our claims. I have a socko solution. We'll stop making claims."

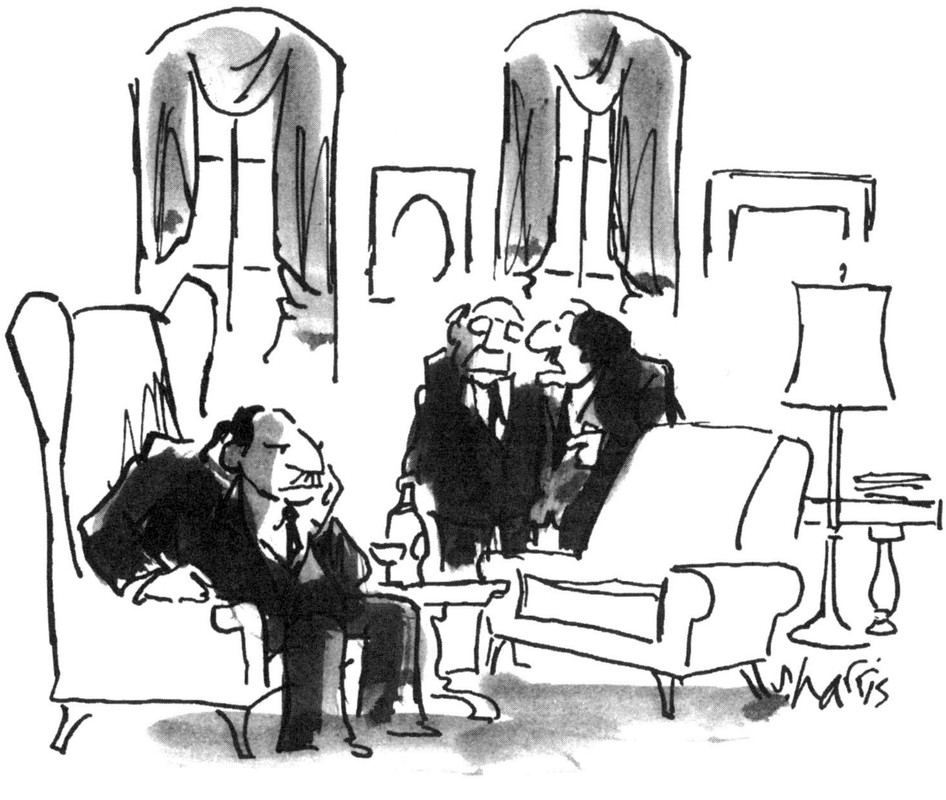

W. Harris

"Bascombe has put all his mutual fund assets into a blind trust, but it was set up so well he can't even locate it."

THE ANNEX FUND

LAST MONEY MARKET FOR 8 BLOCKS

S. Harris

"One or two Japanese auto factories, and this town would be back on its feet in no time."

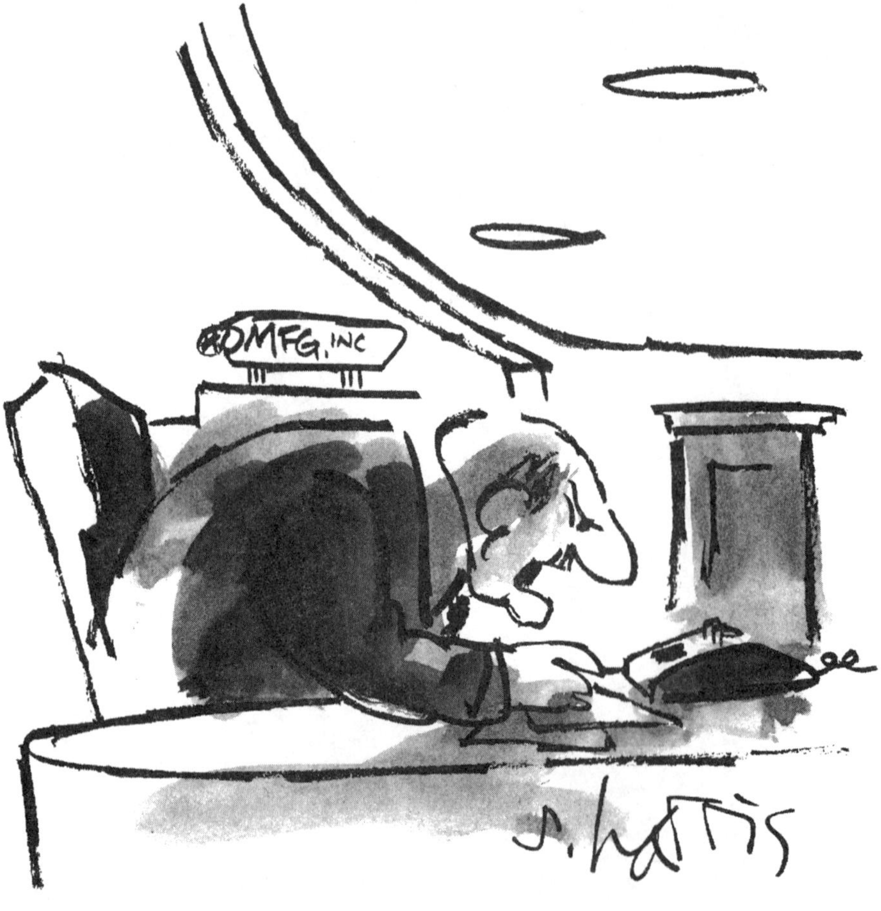
MFG. INC

*"Attention, all department heads!
The buck stops* <u>*there*</u>*. I've had it!"*

"*You can't go wrong. The Futura is a Japanese car made in America, and the Silvette is an American car made in Japan.*"

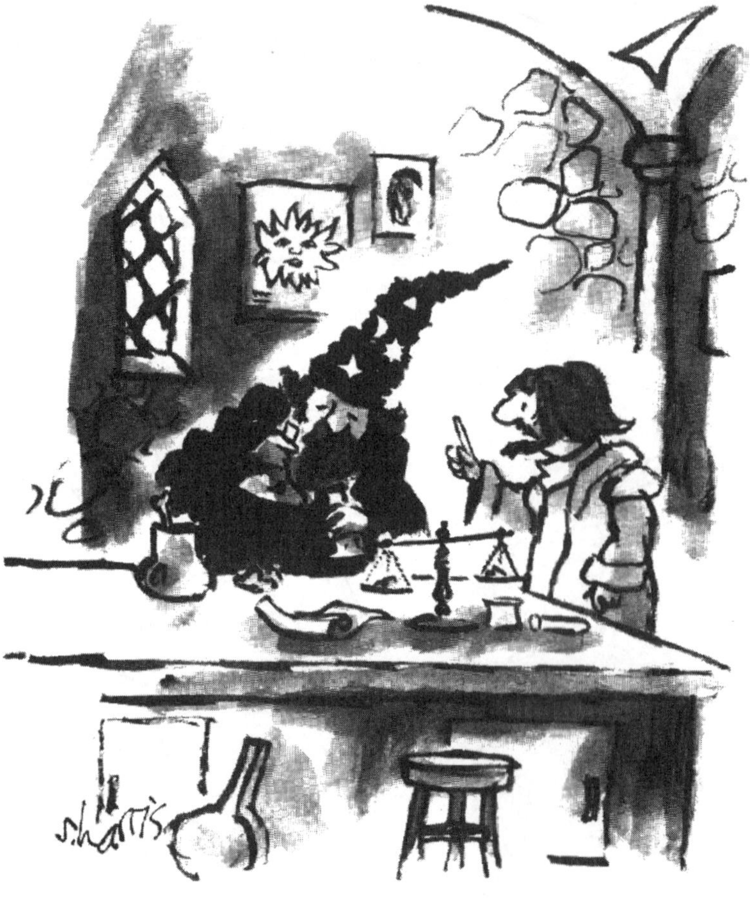
S.harris

"Once you do transmute lead into gold, you'll find the market for it is very speculative."

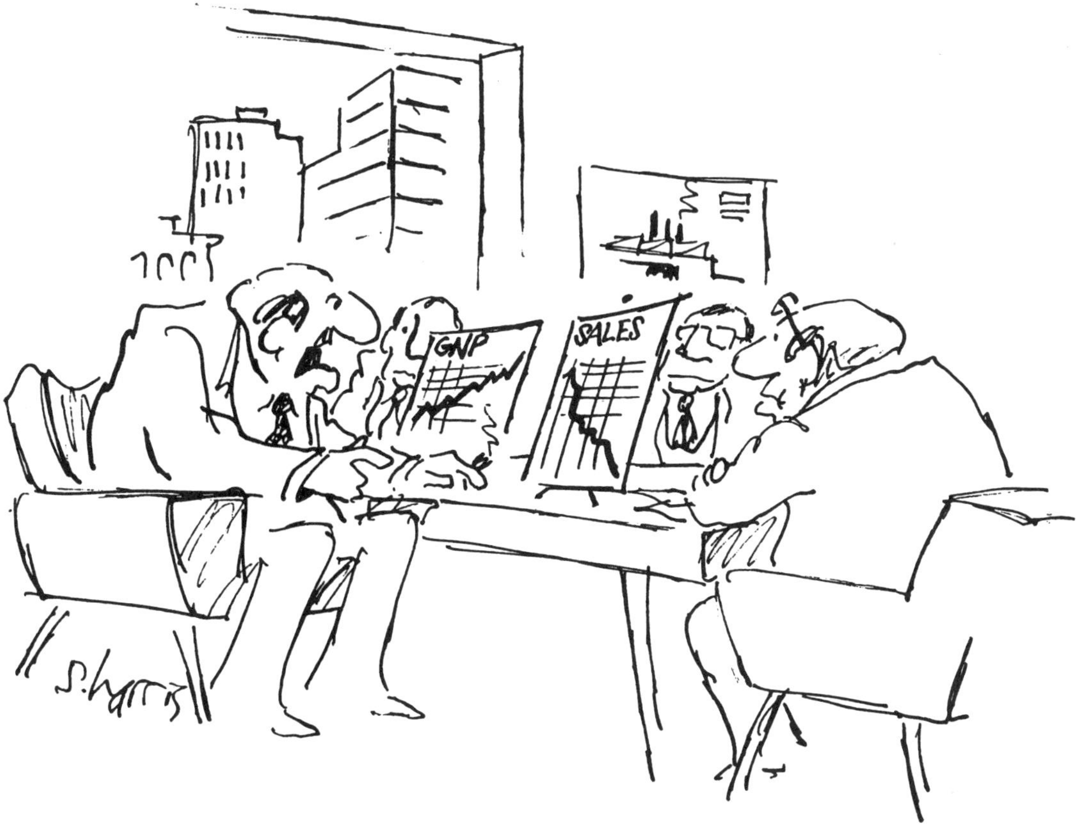
GNP
SALES

"Dammit—How do we get in on that gross national product?"

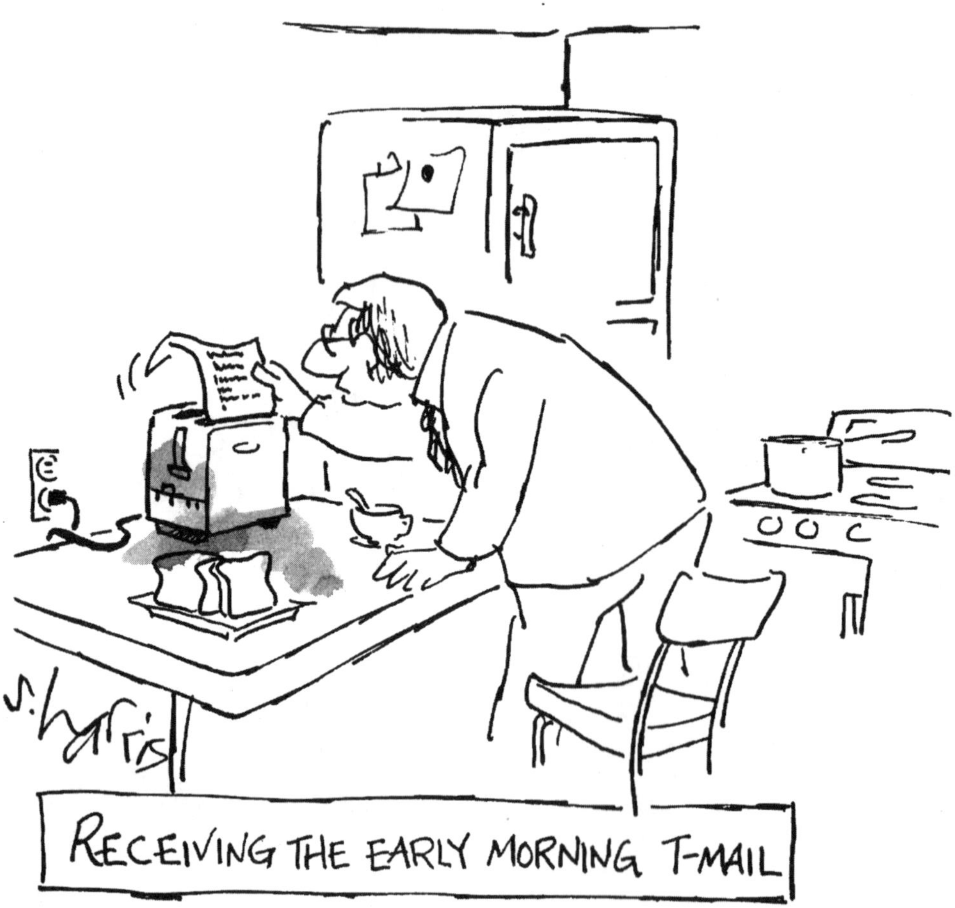
S. Harris

RECEIVING THE EARLY MORNING T-MAIL

"I'll have the businessman-on-the-brink-of-bankruptcy's lunch."

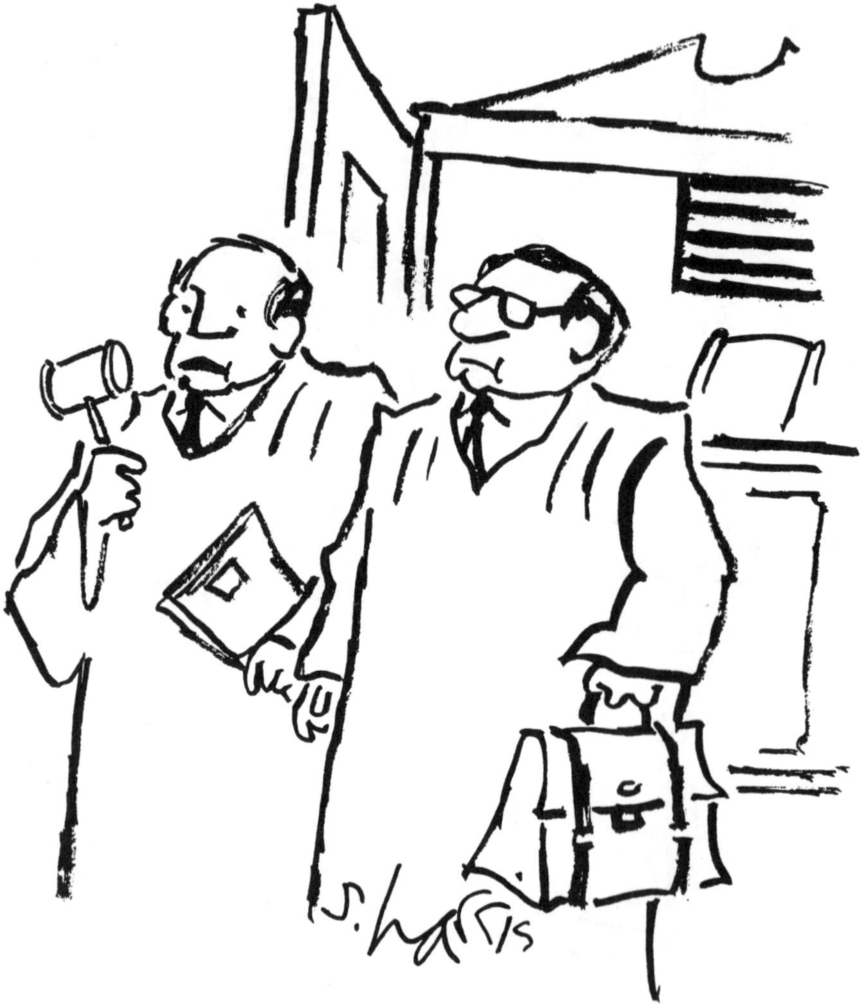
S. Harris

"What really hurt was when I had to divest myself of my holdings in the gavel company."

"Don't let the round table fool you.
Wherever he sits, that the head."

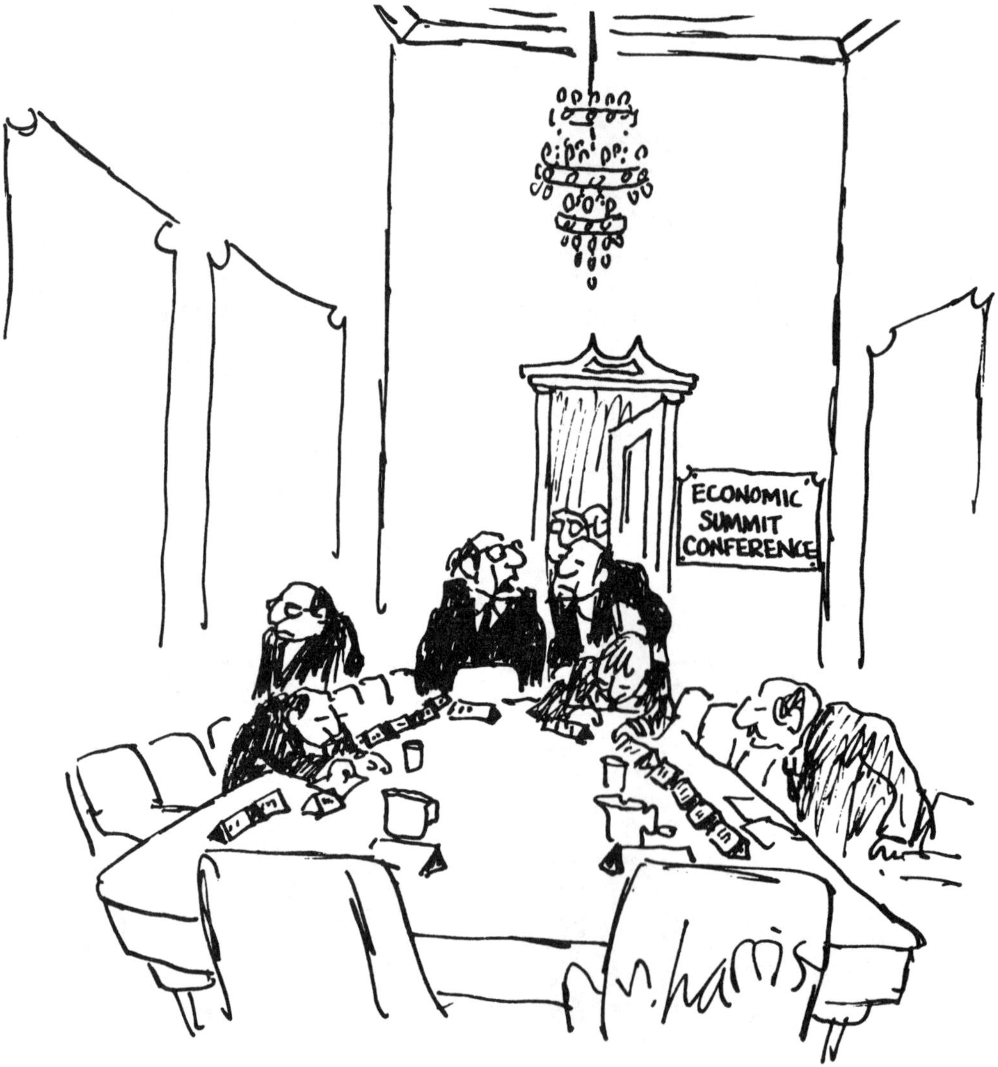
ECONOMIC
SUMMIT
CONFERENCE

*"Is it good money that drives out bad,
or bad money that drives out good?"*

"It's alright to do your regular work, Sanders, but haven't you caught on yet? The big money is in breakthroughs."

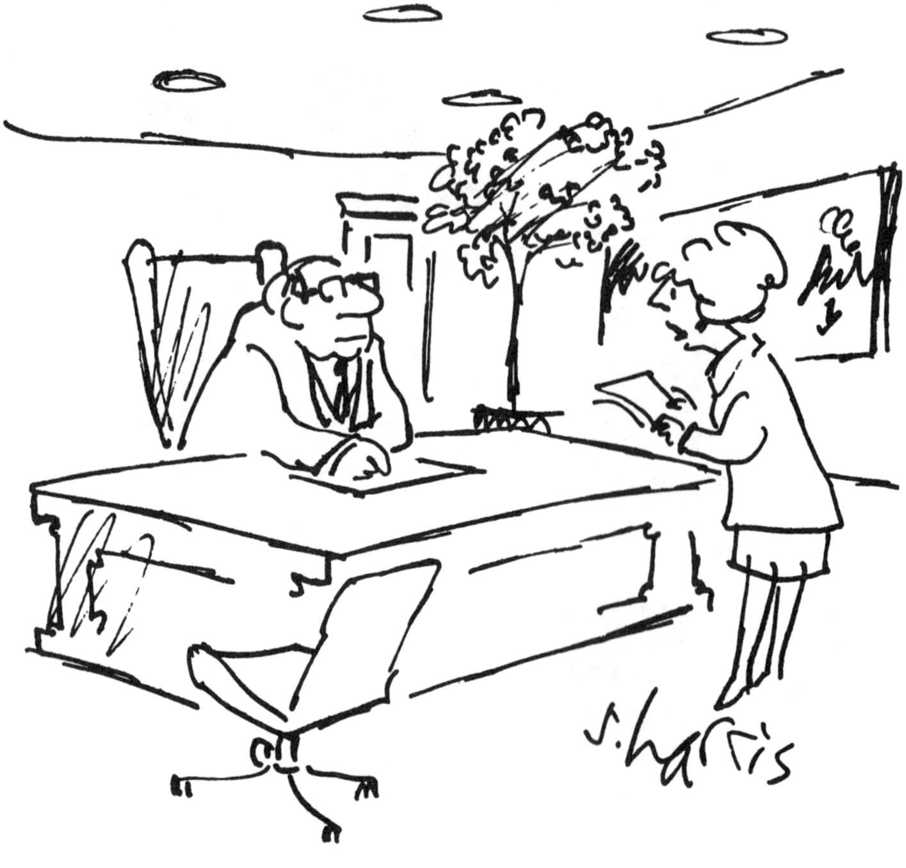
S. Harris

"This morning a rumor that we would buy the Arpex Corp. drove our stock up $3. Around noon a rumor that Arpex would buy us drove it up another $3. And in the afternoon a rumor that we have nothing to do with Arpex drove it up $3 more."

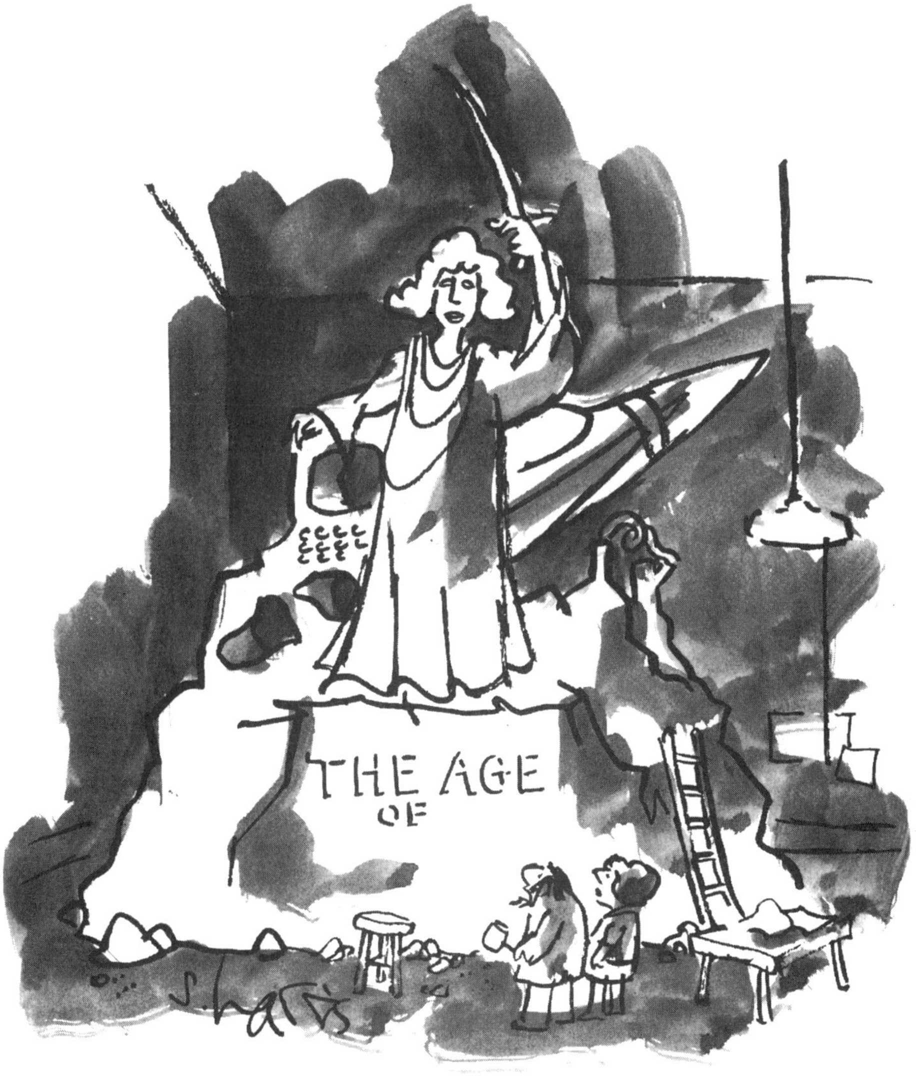
THE AGE
OF

"What the hell is this the age of?"

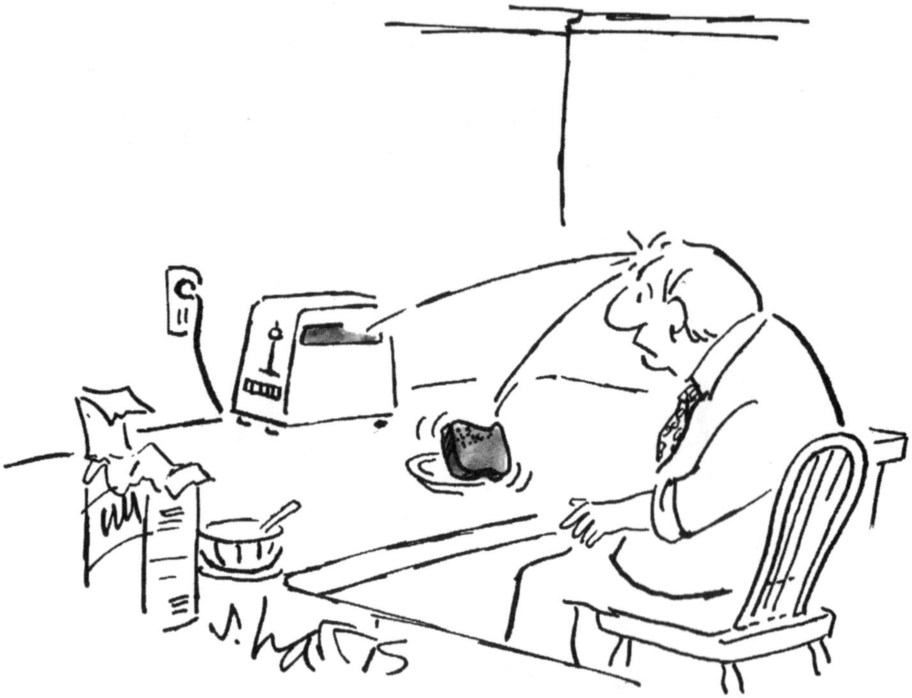
S. harris

THE INTERACTIVE TOASTER

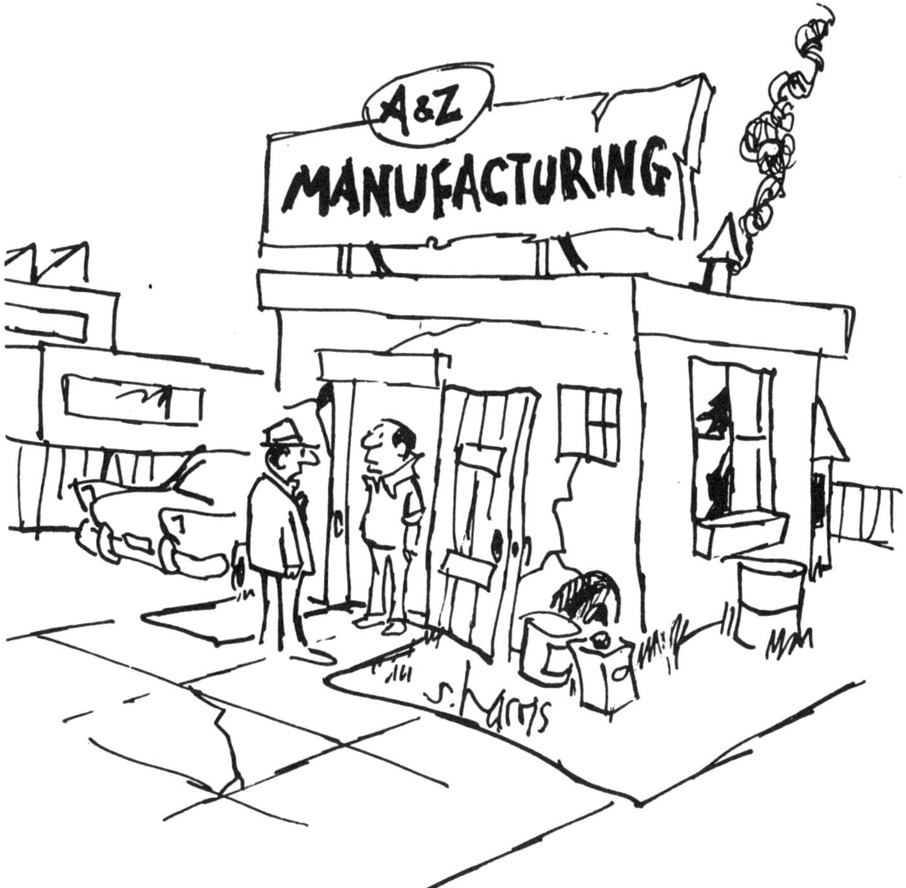
A&Z
MANUFACTURING

"So that's why your stock sells at 36,000 times earnings."

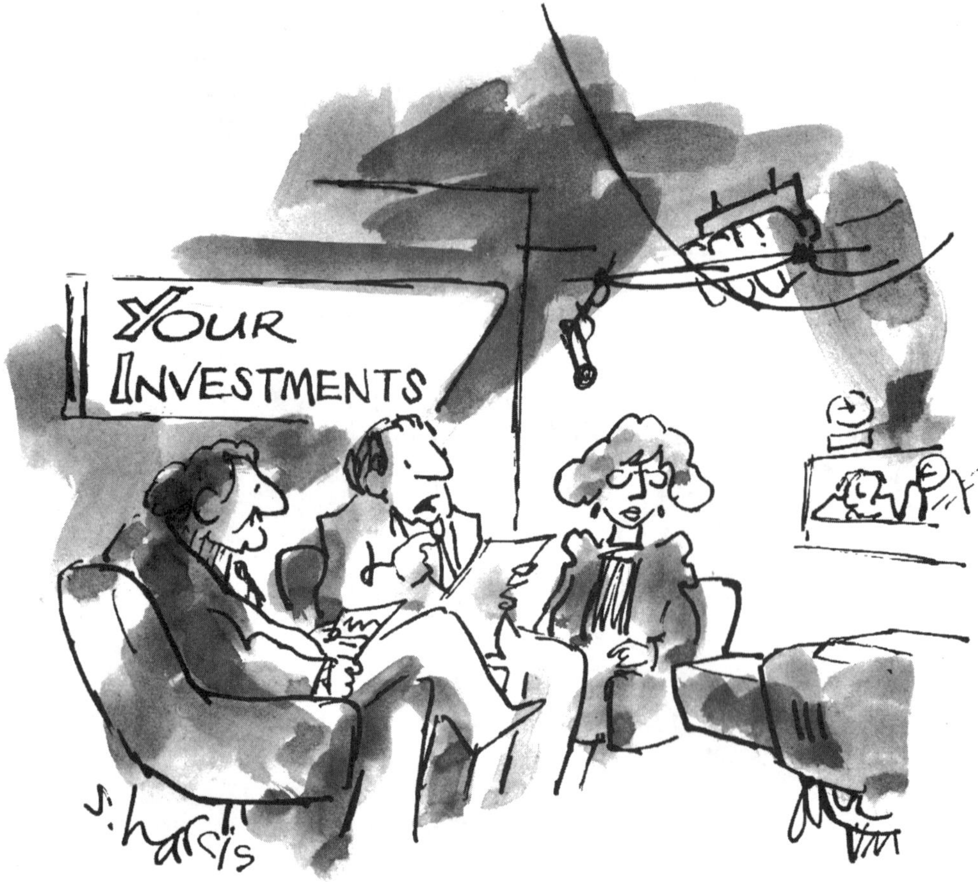
YOUR INVESTMENTS

". . . and if you have been following our advice every week, you should just about be wiped out by now."

"What's going on here? What _you_ see is what
_I_ get, and what _I_ see is what _you_ get."

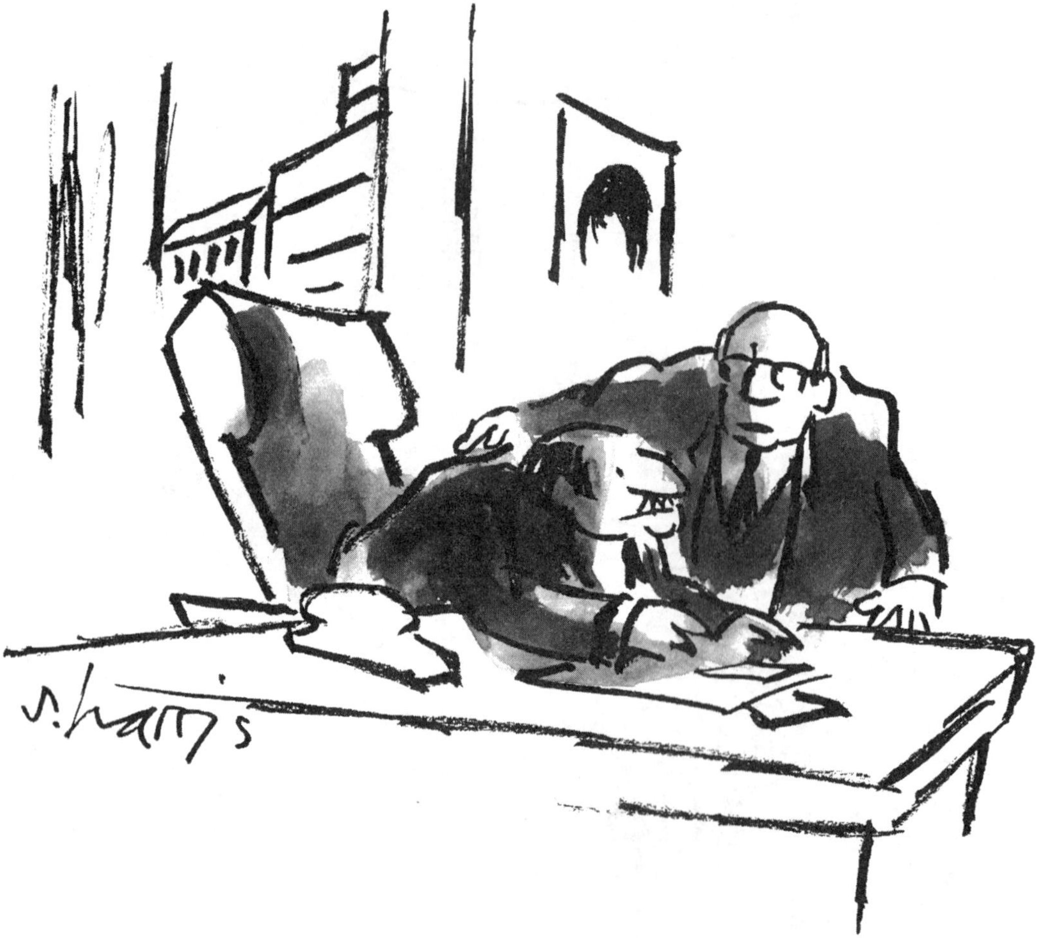
S. harris

*"But R.G., you can't be a big fish in all the big ponds—
you can only be a big fish in your big pond."*

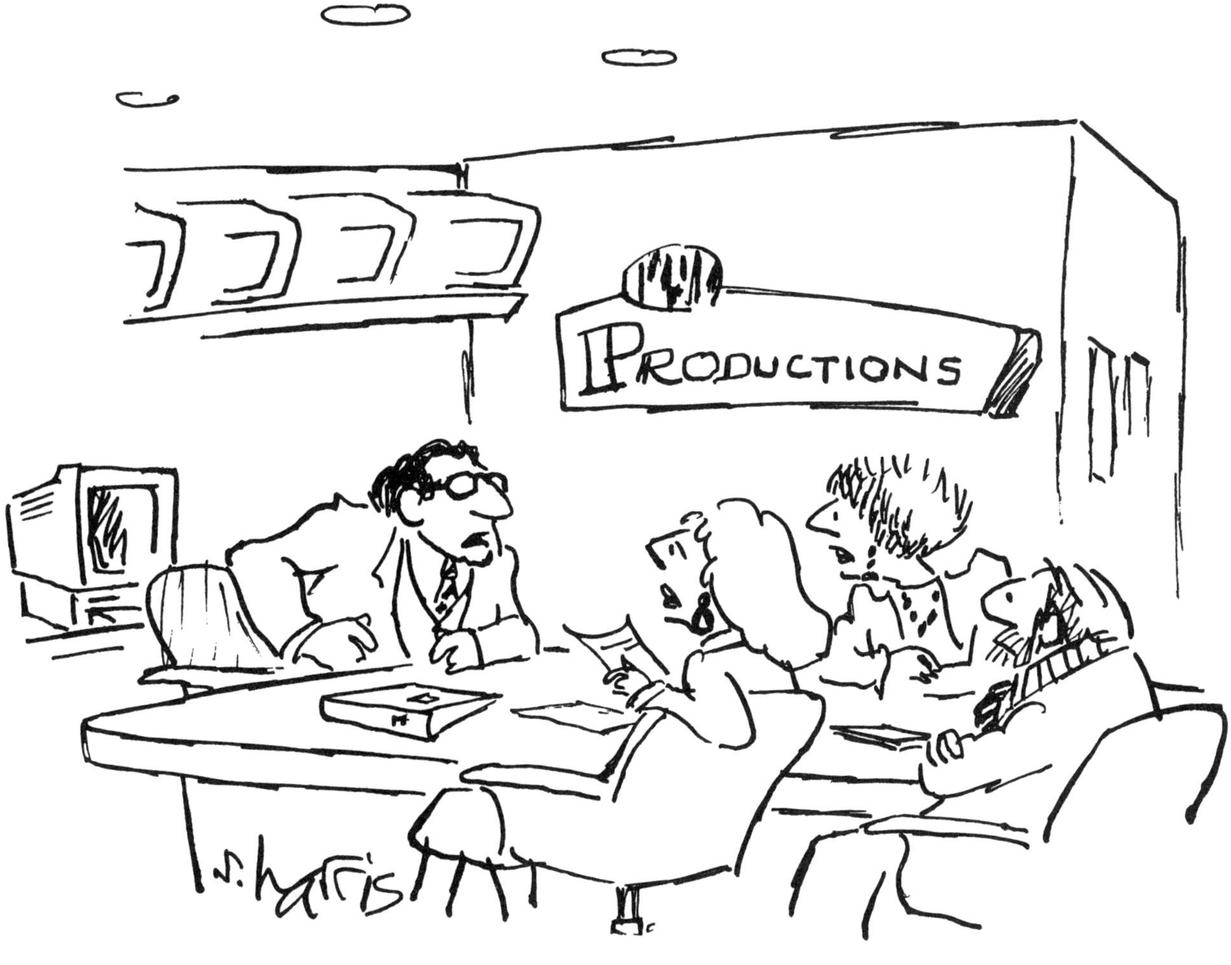
PRODUCTIONS

"There's a thin line between good taste and bad taste. Does anyone know where that line is?"

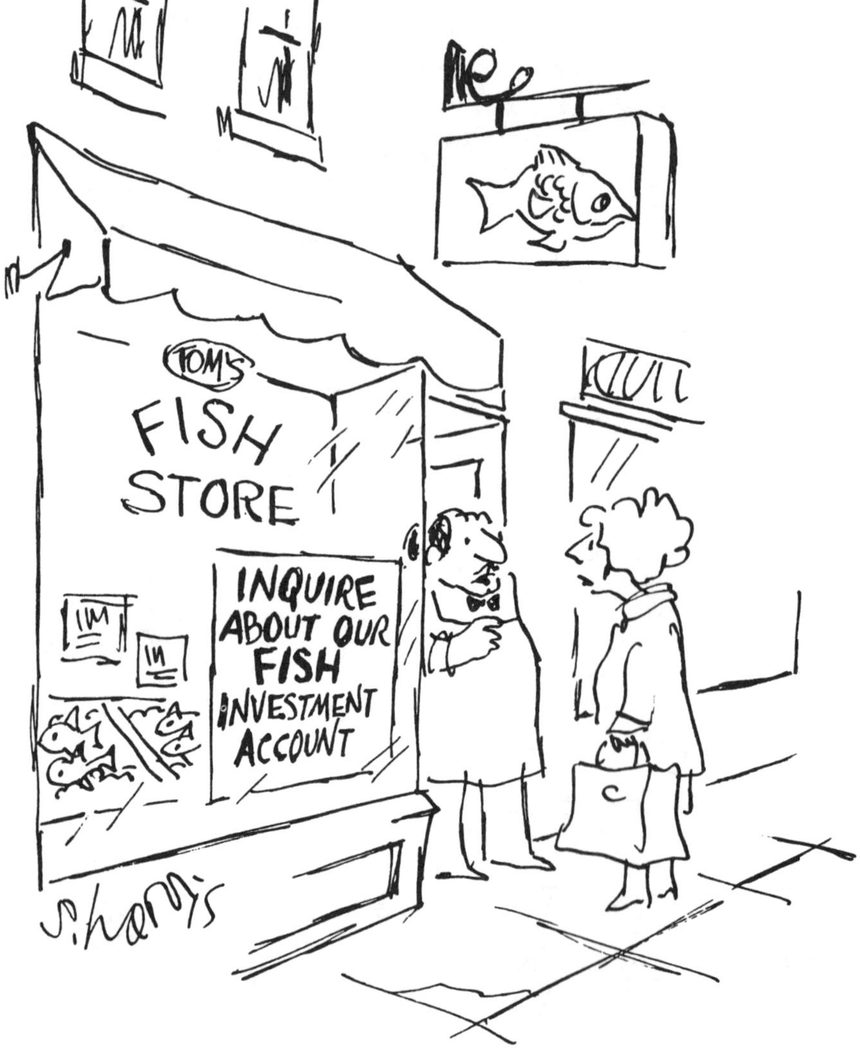
TOM'S
FISH STORE
INQUIRE ABOUT OUR FISH INVESTMENT ACCOUNT
S. Harris

"You simply put up a minimum of $2,500. If the price of fish goes up, your investment goes up. If the price of the fish goes down, your investment goes down."

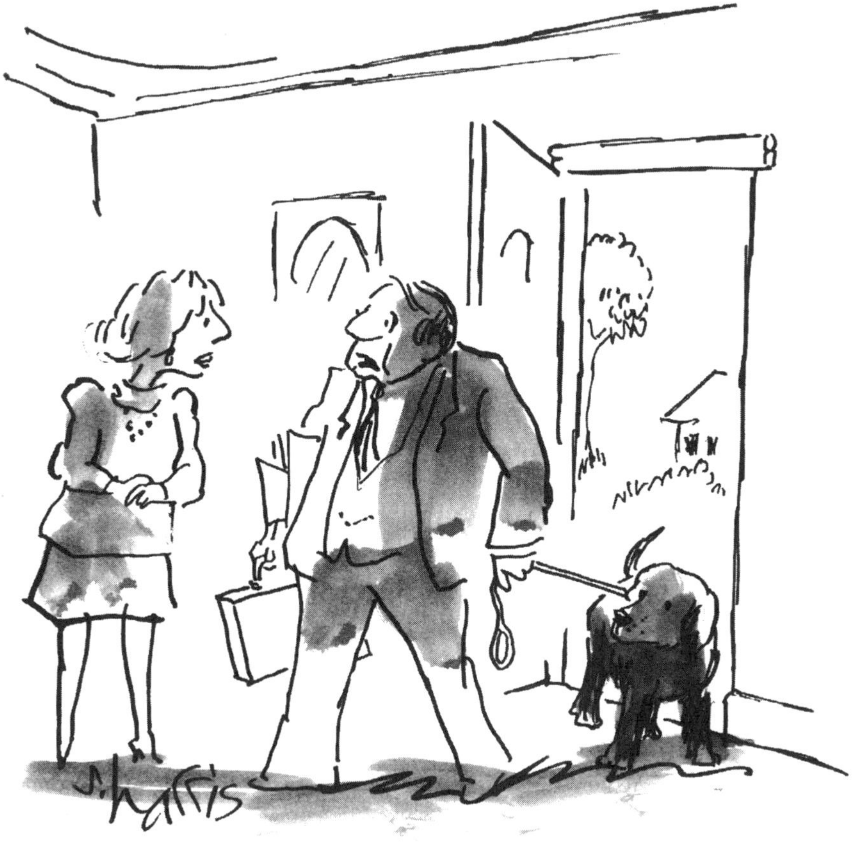
S. Harris

"Dexter got a golden parachute, Nolan got a golden handshake and I got a golden retriever."

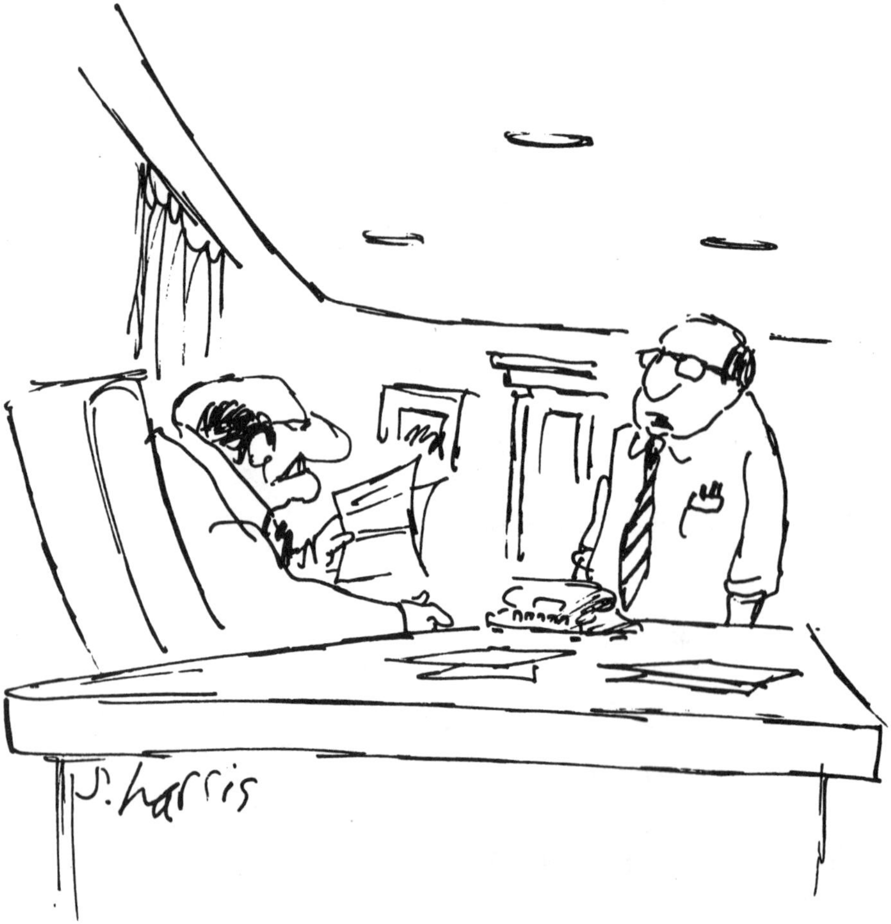
S.harris

"I didn't say I majored in business administration—
I said I took business administration."

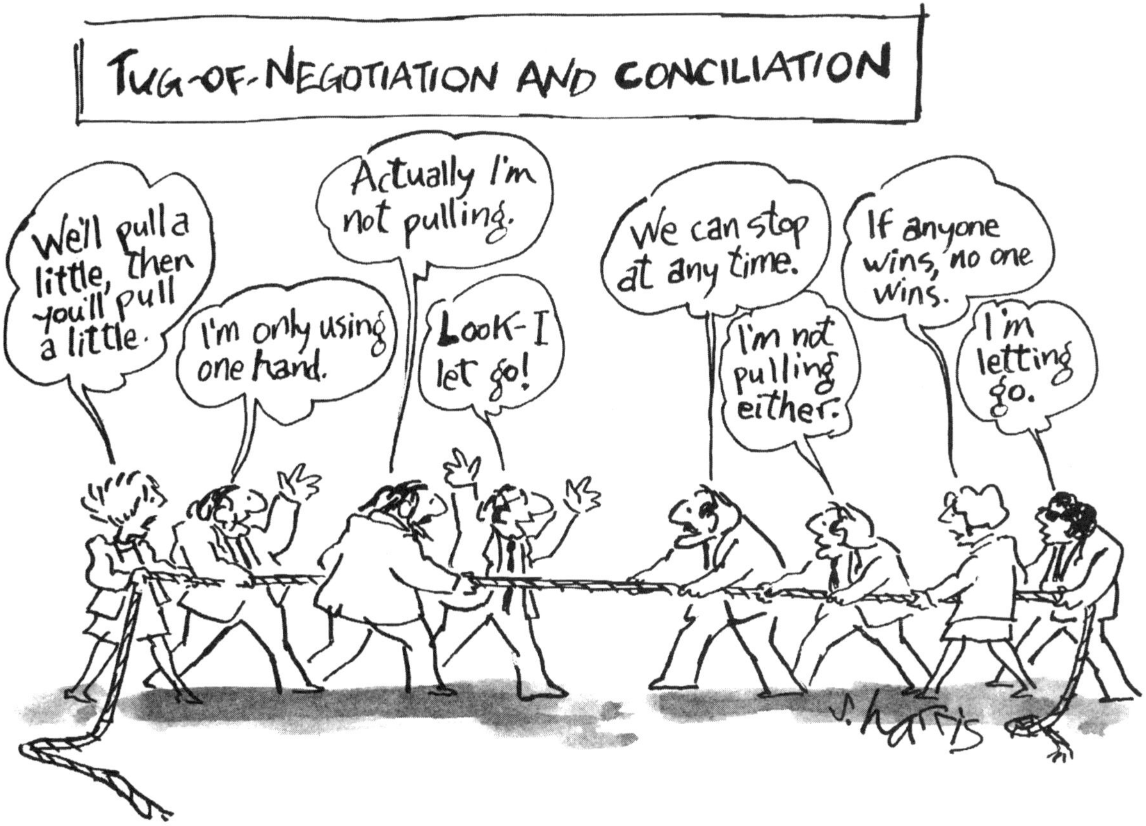
TUG-OF-NEGOTIATION AND CONCILIATION
We'll pull a little, then you'll pull a little.
I'm only using one hand.
Actually I'm not pulling.
Look- I let go!
We can stop at any time.
I'm not pulling either.
If anyone wins, no one wins.
I'm letting go.
S. Harris

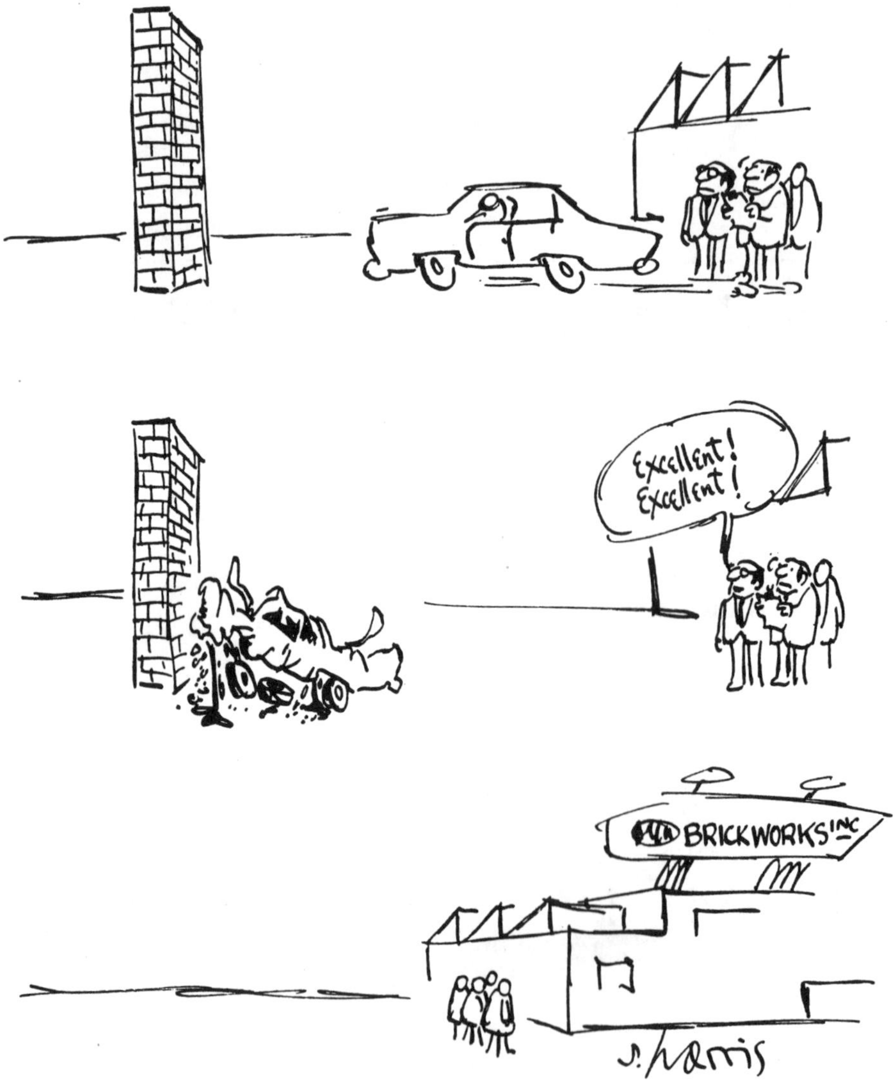
Excellent!
Excellent!
BRICKWORKS INC
S. Harris

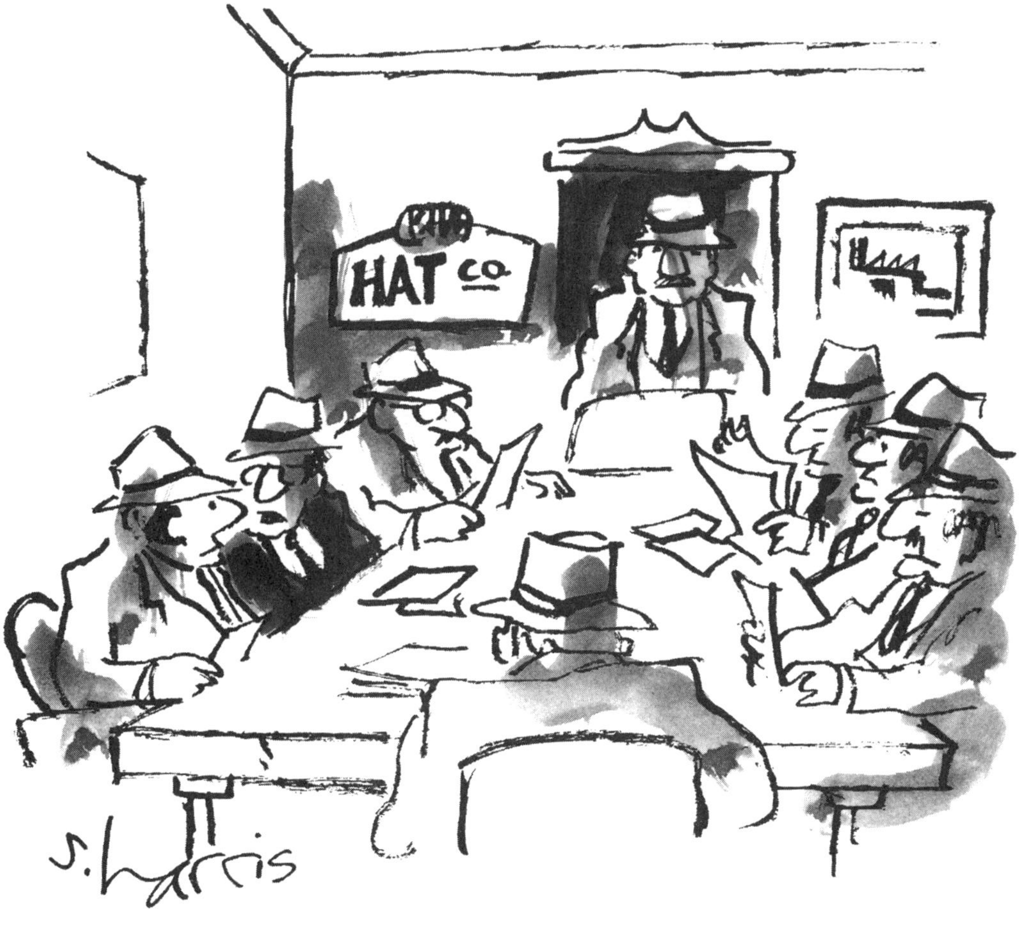
HAT CO.

"Whatever you do, never say anything about being warm."

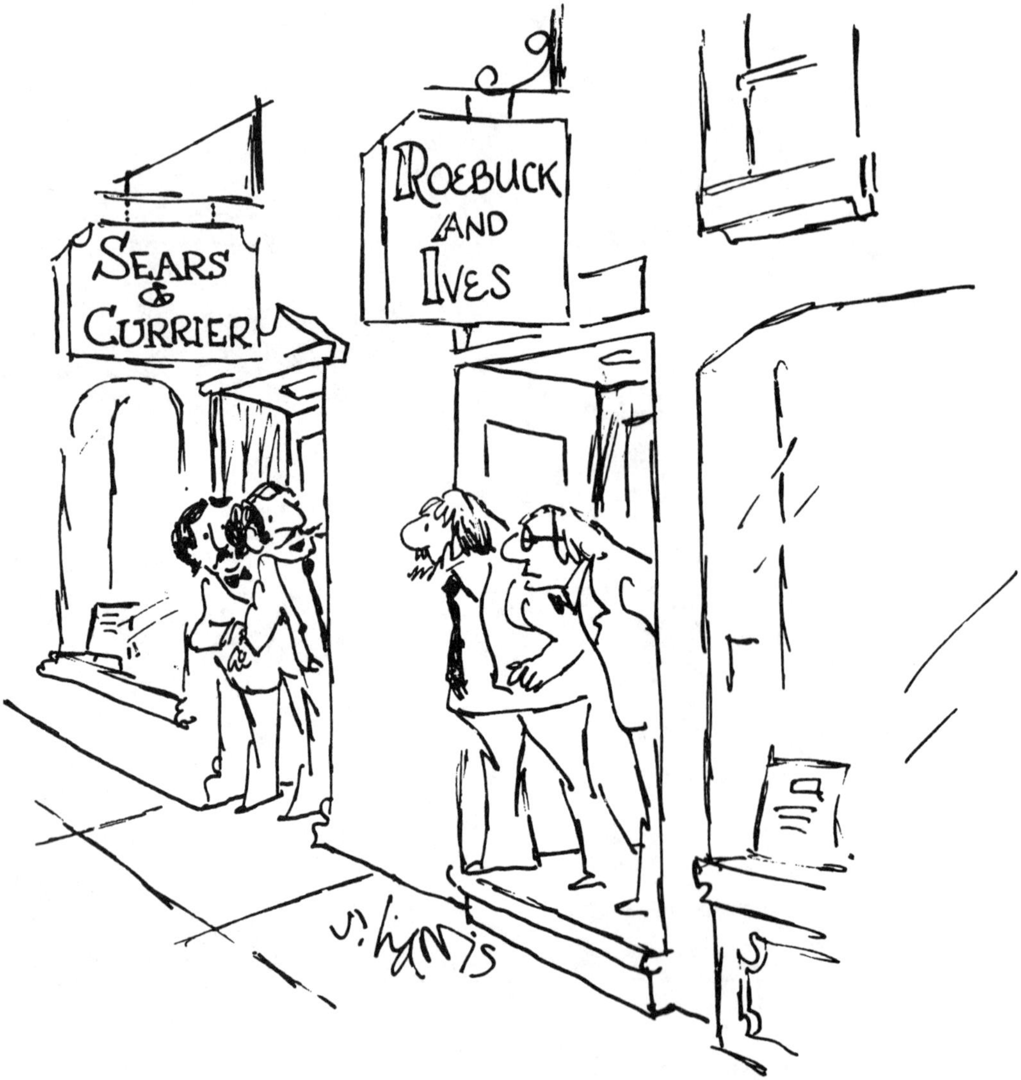
SEARS & CURRIER
ROEBUCK AND IVES

"We have what might be a very good idea . . ."

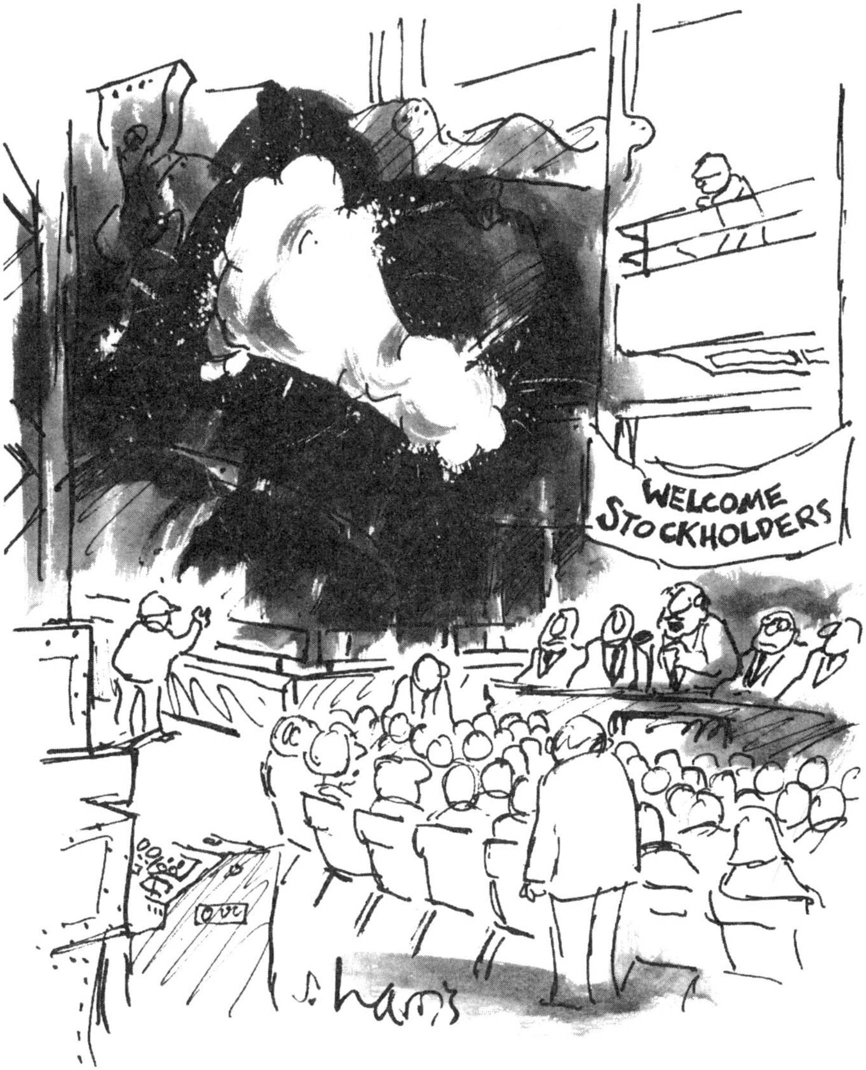
WELCOME STOCKHOLDERS
S. Harris

"Some of you were wondering, 'What, exactly, does Smedgwick Refining and Smelting do?' . . ."

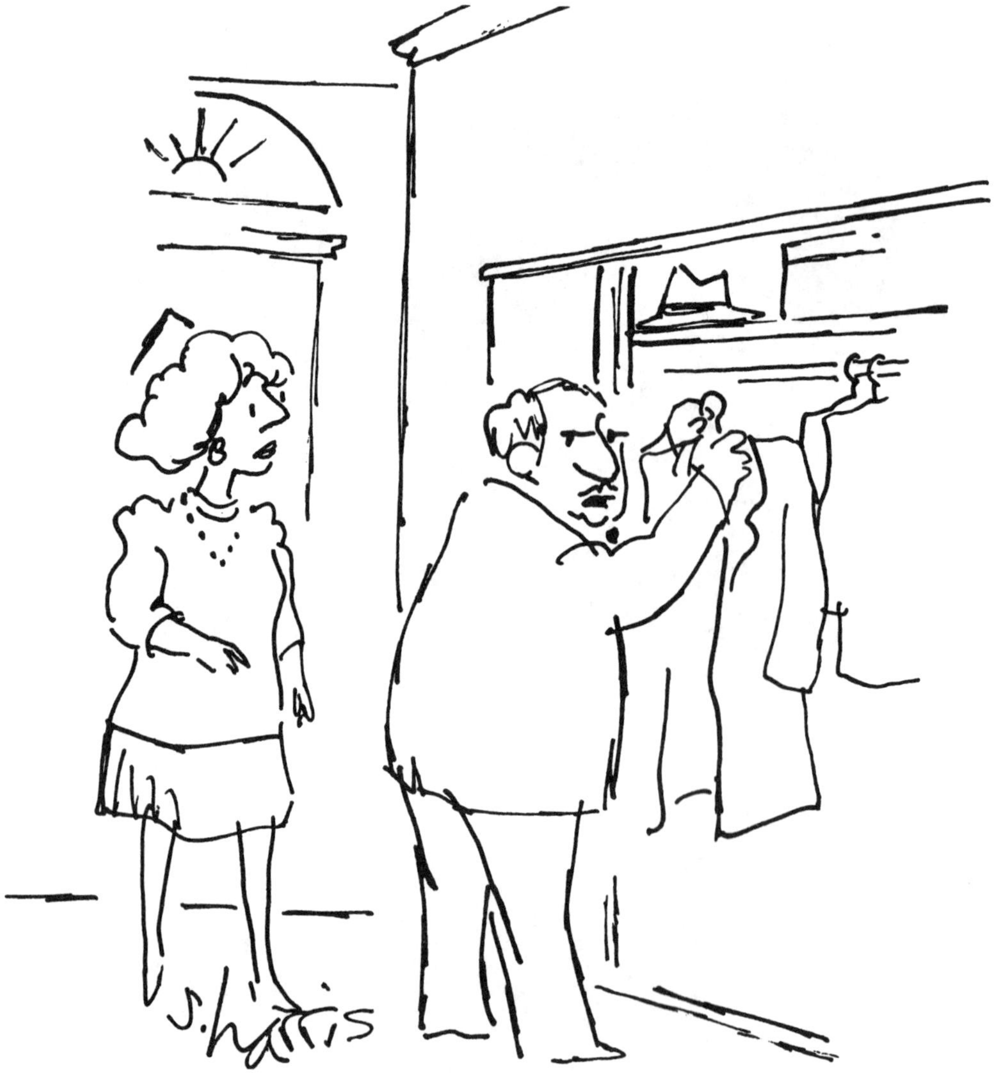
S. Harris

"I heard it's harmful for a person to keep his hostility bottled up, so I fired everybody."

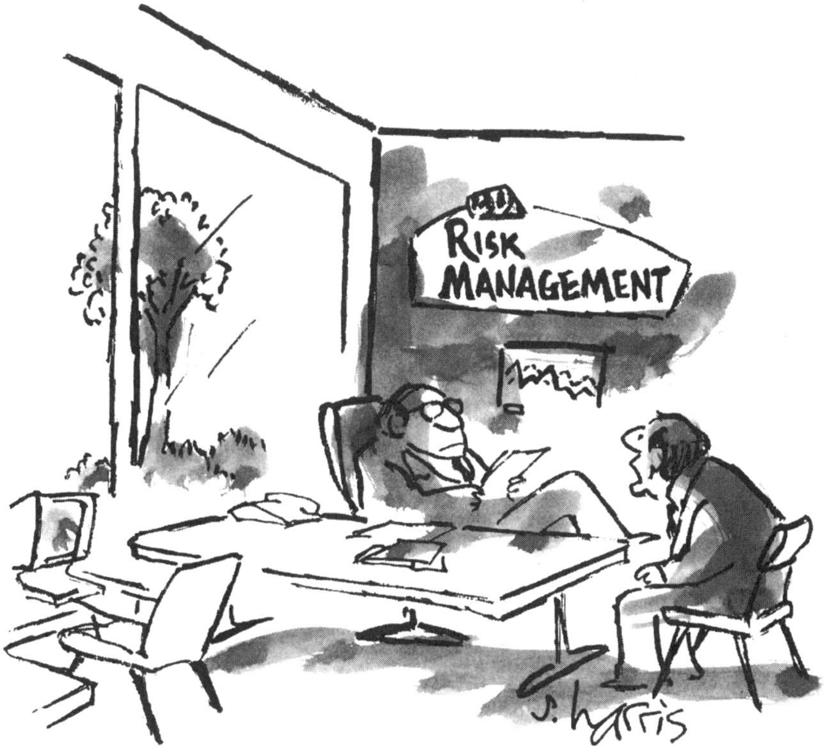
RISK MANAGEMENT

"'Be careful'! All you can tell me is 'be careful'?"

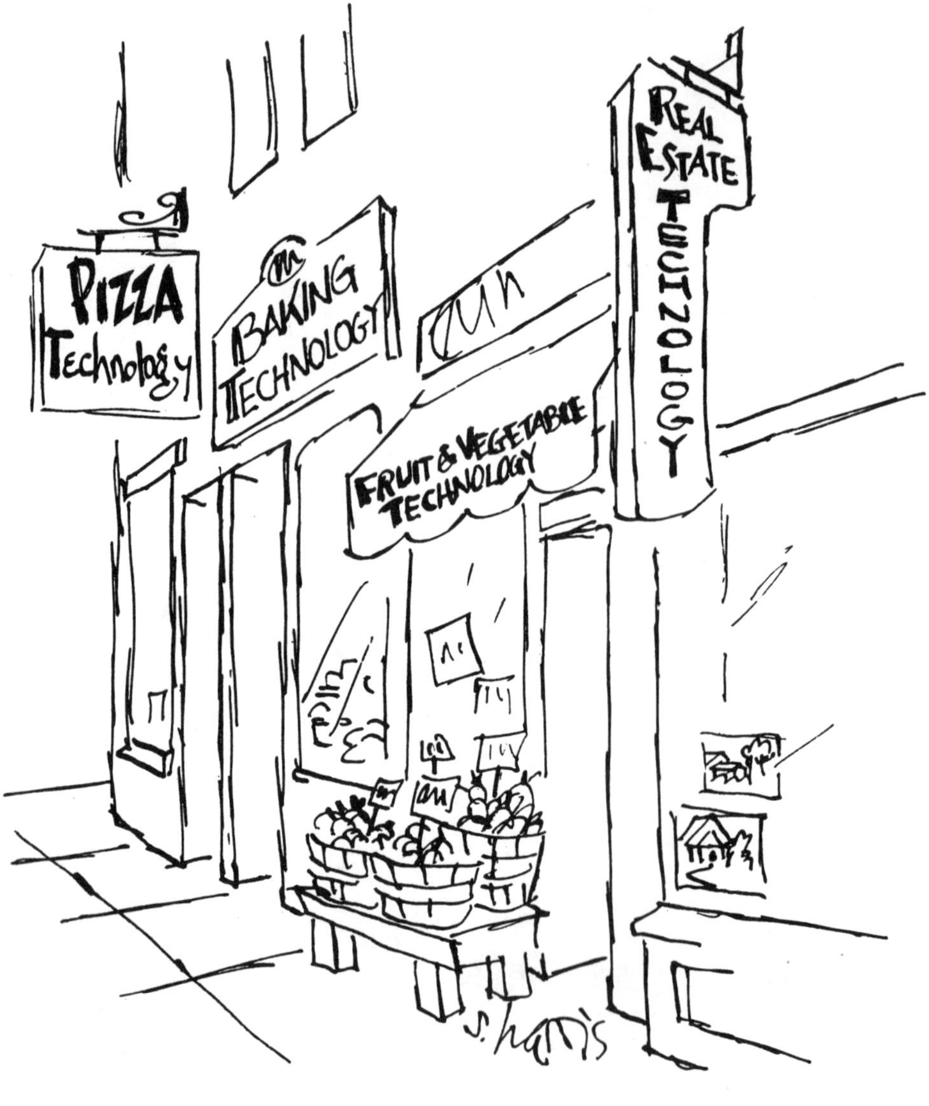
PIZZA
Technology
BAKING
TECHNOLOGY
FRUIT & VEGETABLE
TECHNOLOGY
REAL
ESTATE
TECHNOLOGY
S. Harris

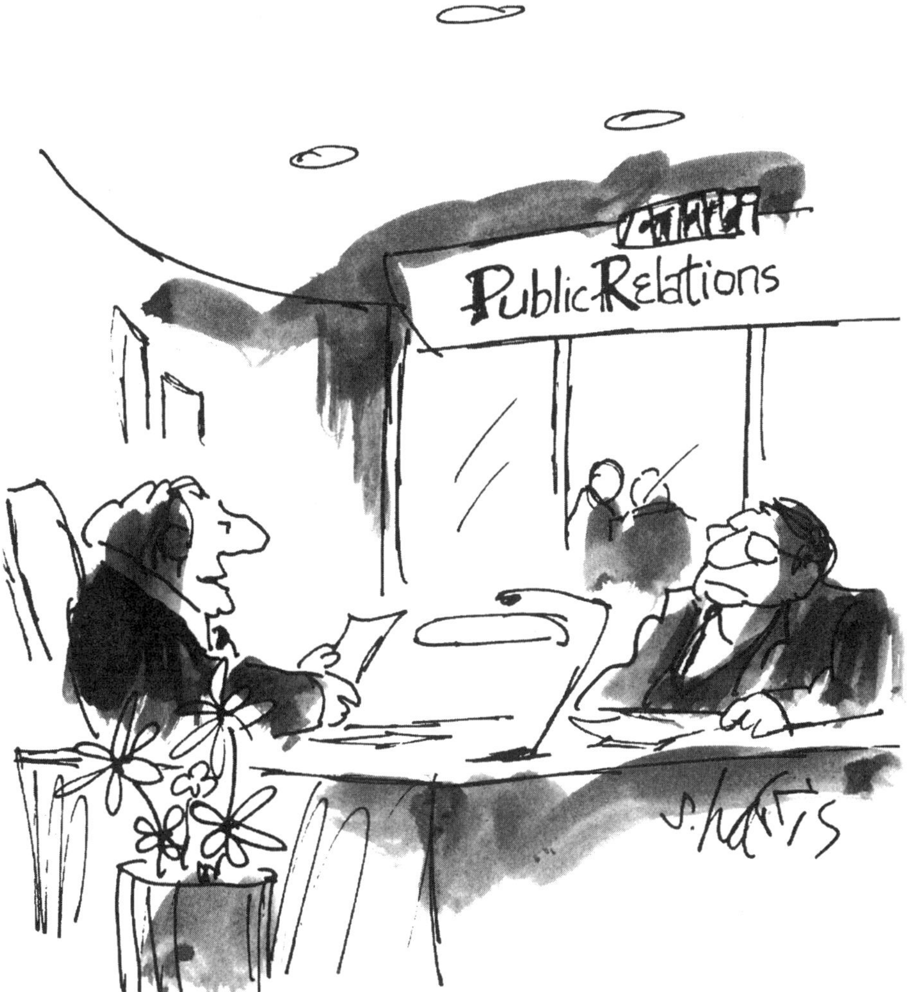
Public Relations

". . . and if your recognition-factor begins to slip, sirens will go off in seven critical media centers."

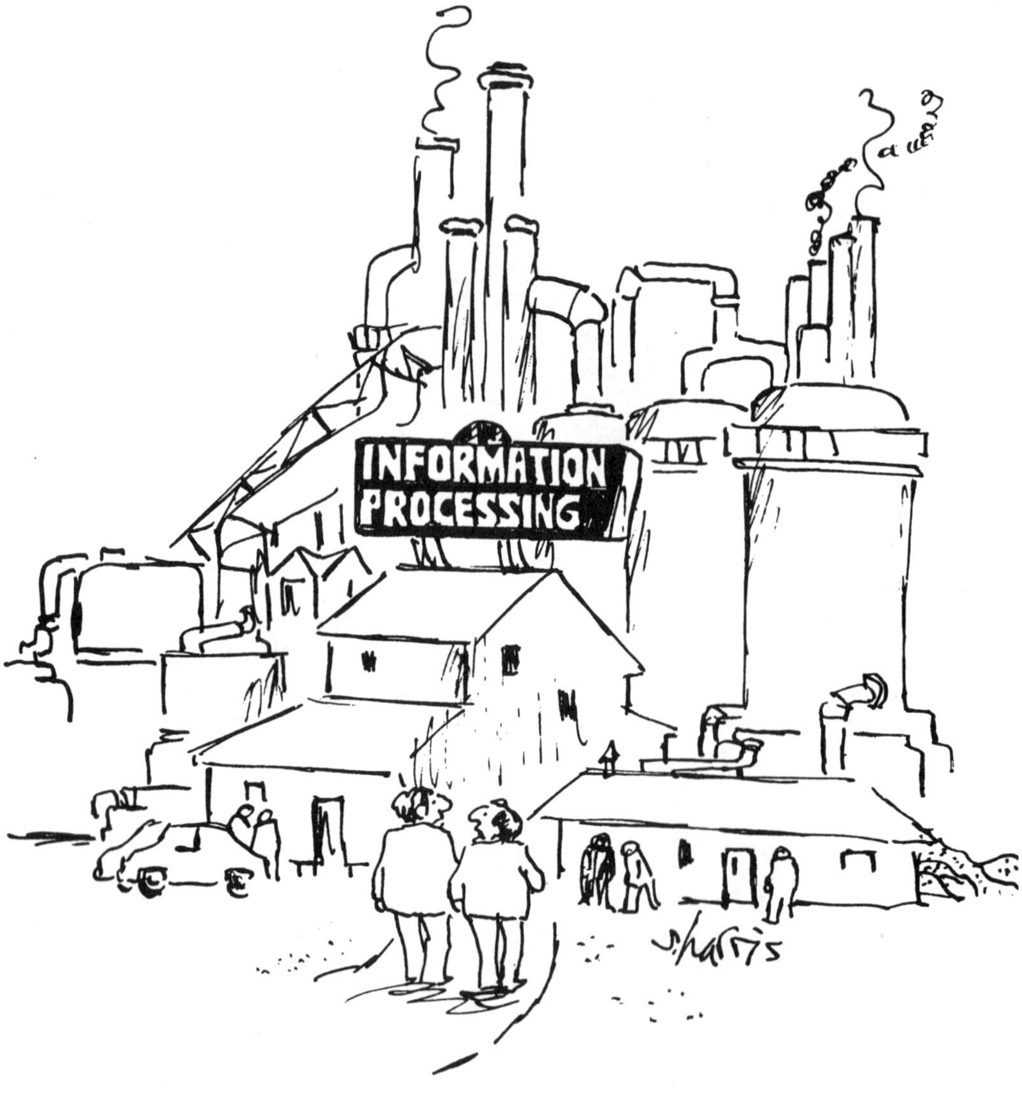
INFORMATION
PROCESSING

*"Back in the industrial age, this was,
I believe, a steel mill."*

"Sure, real estate prices are sky-high, but kings don't sell their castles, and that's that."

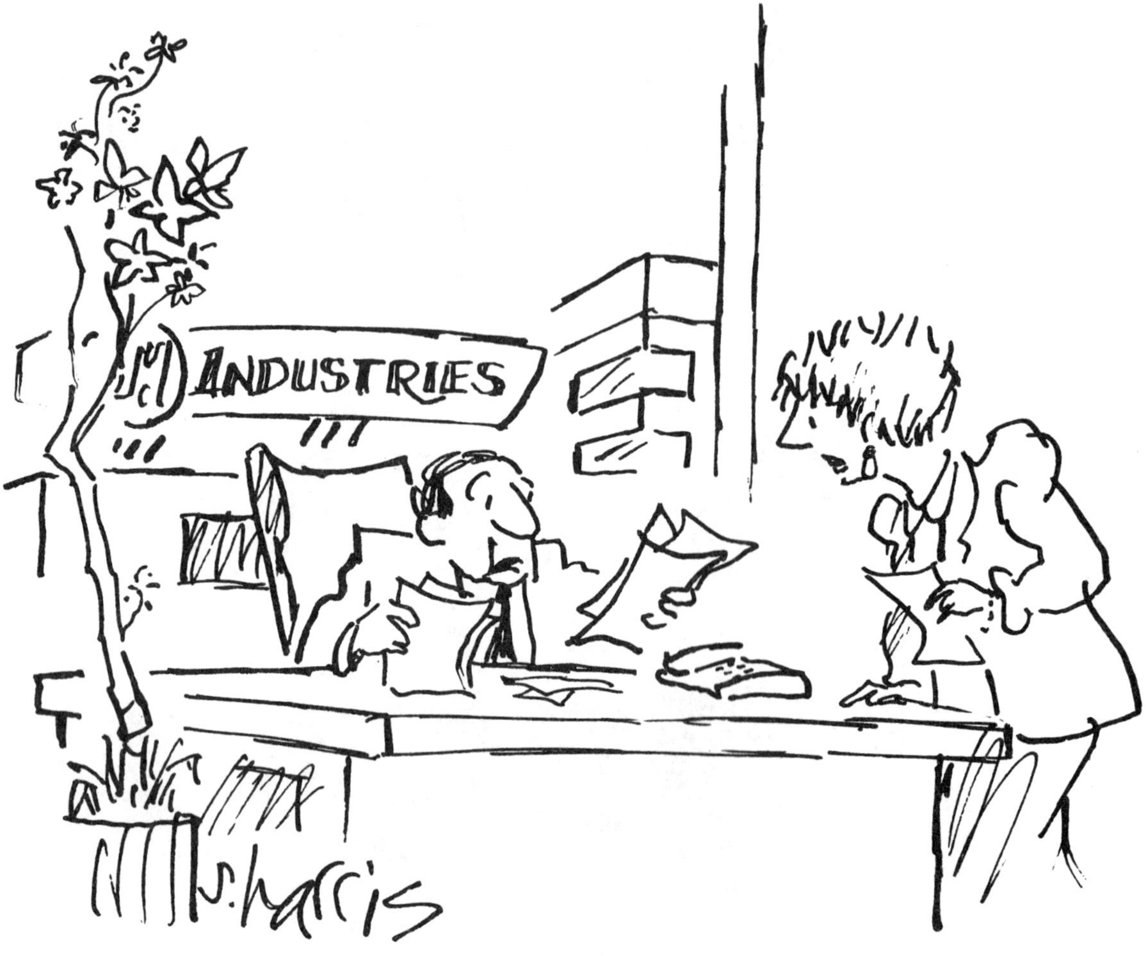
INDUSTRIES
S. Harris

"We divested ourselves of a division here, a subsidiary there, a branch here, an affiliate there . . . there's nothing left!"

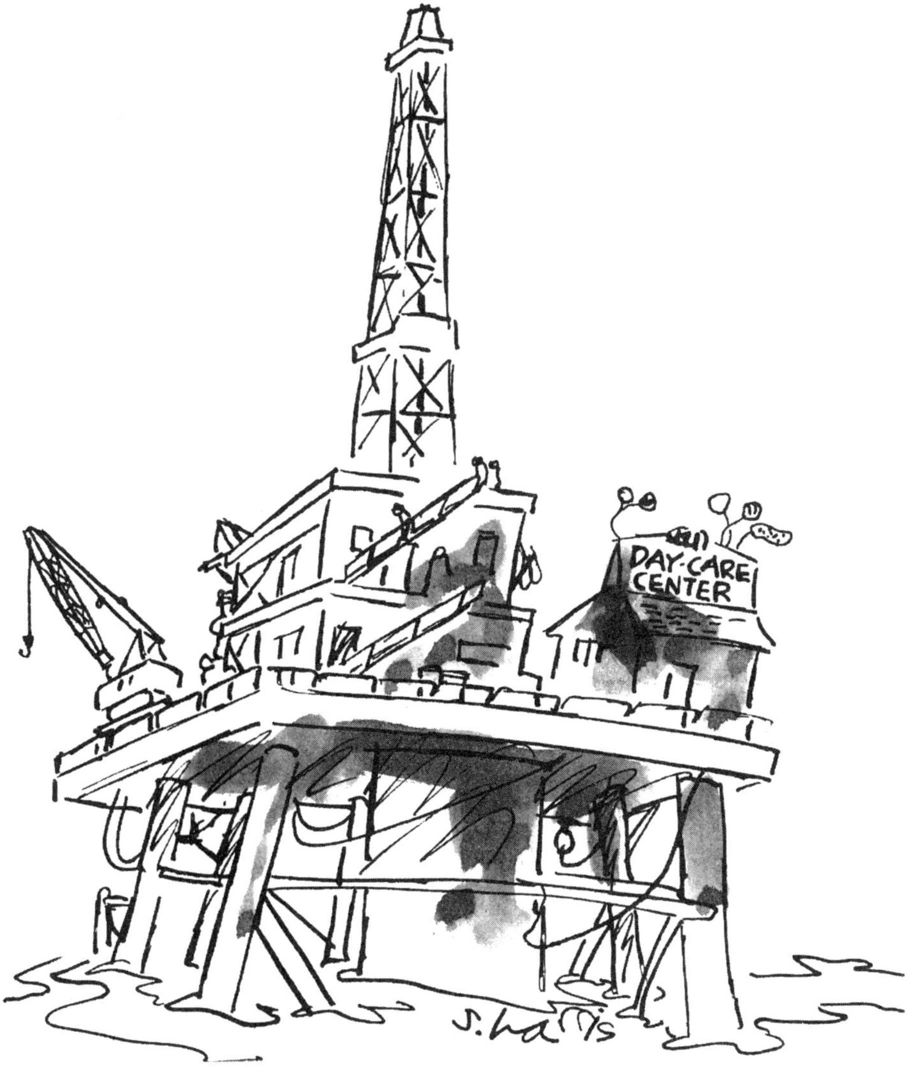
DAY-CARE
CENTER
S. Harris

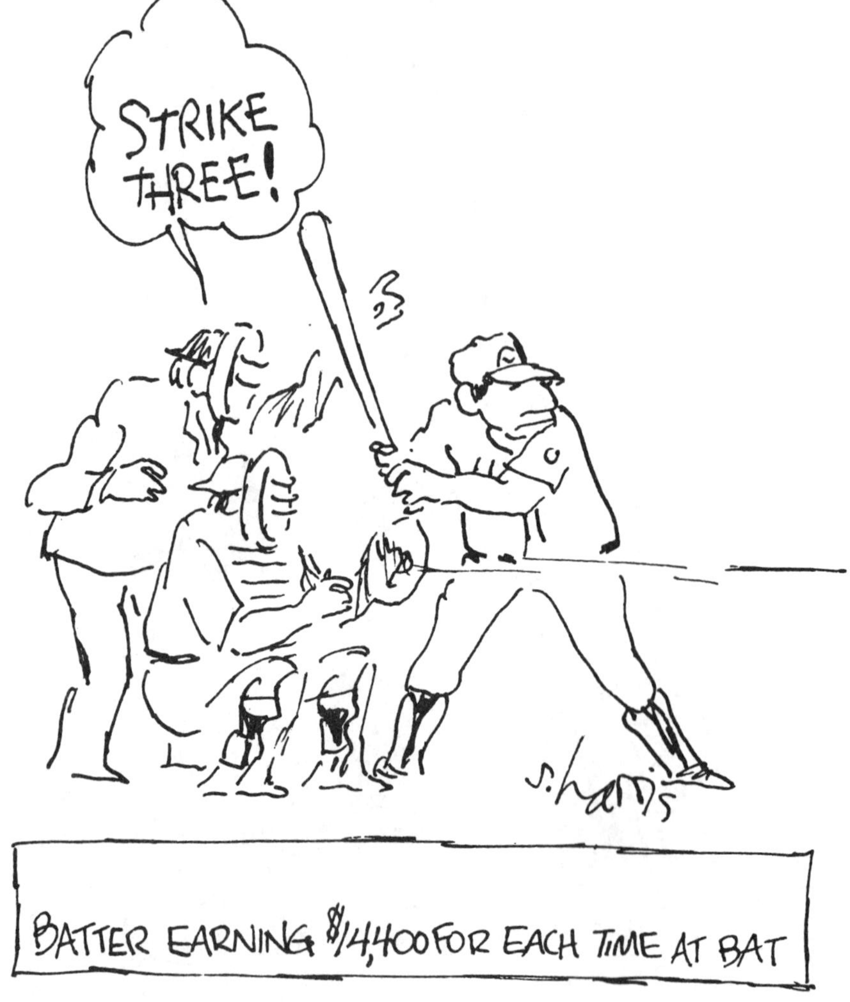
STRIKE THREE!
s.harris

BATTER EARNING $14,400 FOR EACH TIME AT BAT

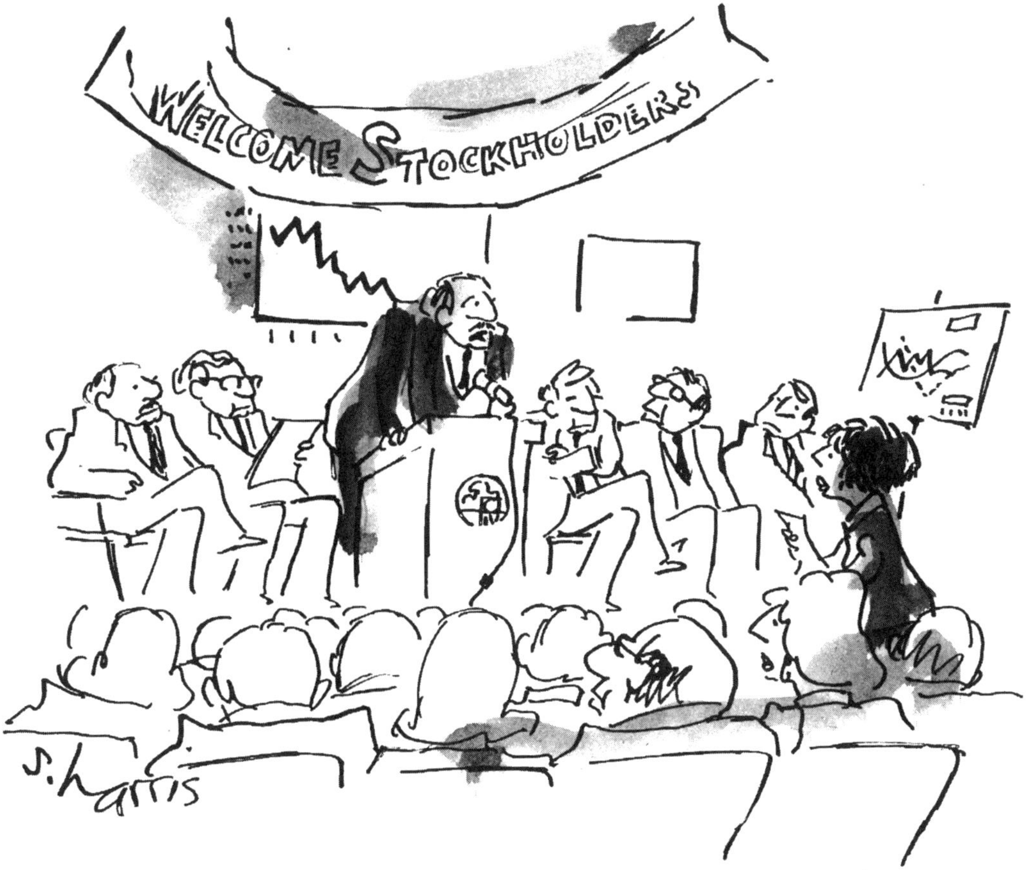
WELCOME STOCKHOLDERS
S. Harris

"We <u>did</u> invite some women to be on the board. They wanted no part of it."

"I took my money out of the bank, and put it into municipal bonds.
Then I went into a money market. Shortly thereafter,
I put everything into commodities, and then into the stock
market. Now it's in gold and silver. However, all the
commissions have nearly wiped me out."

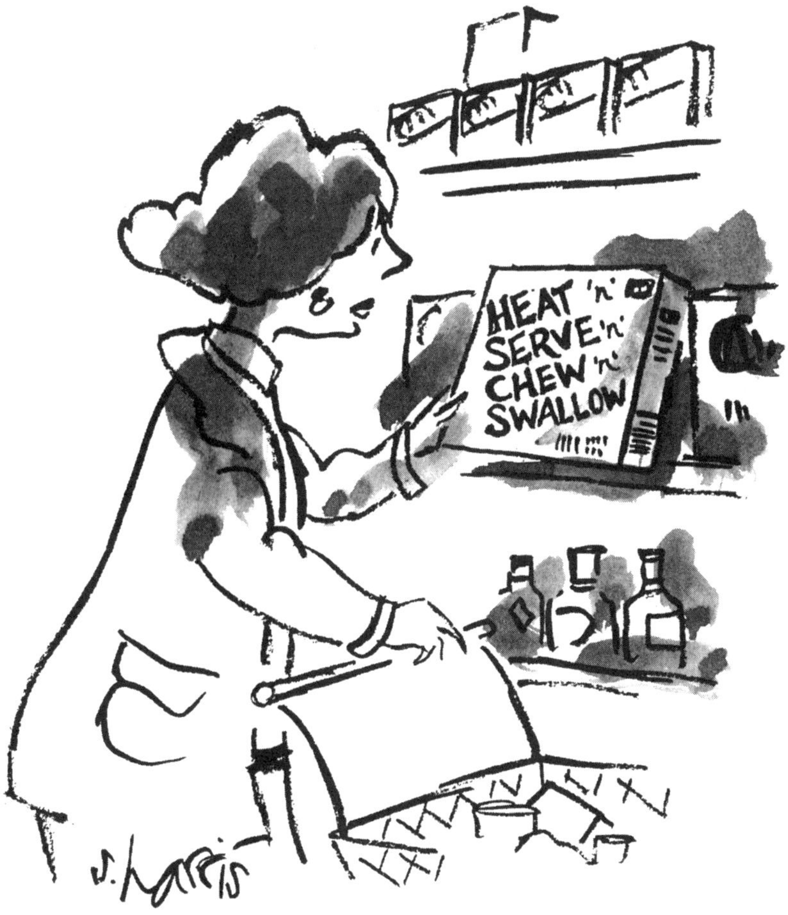
HEAT 'n' SERVE 'n' CHEW 'n' SWALLOW
S. Harris

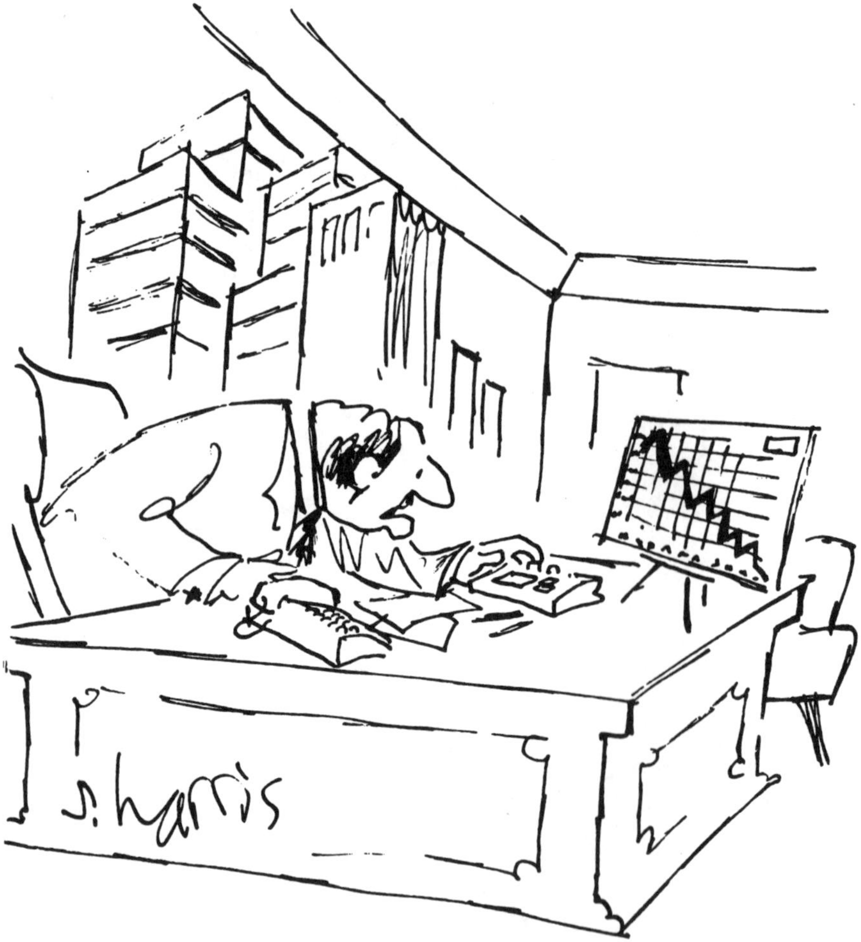
S. Harris

"Ms. Kaye, send in the company optimist."

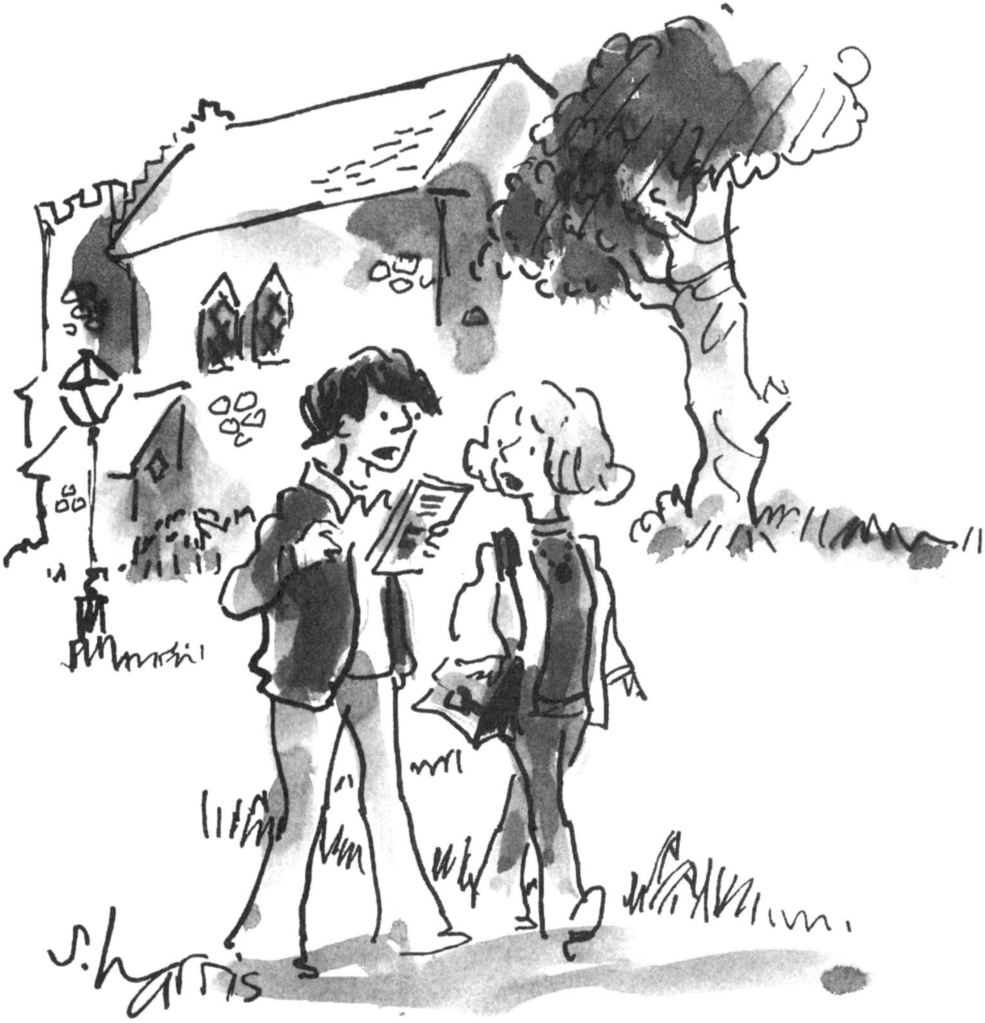
S. Harris

"Now they're talking! This semester, the list of courses mentions how much each could add to your income after graduation."

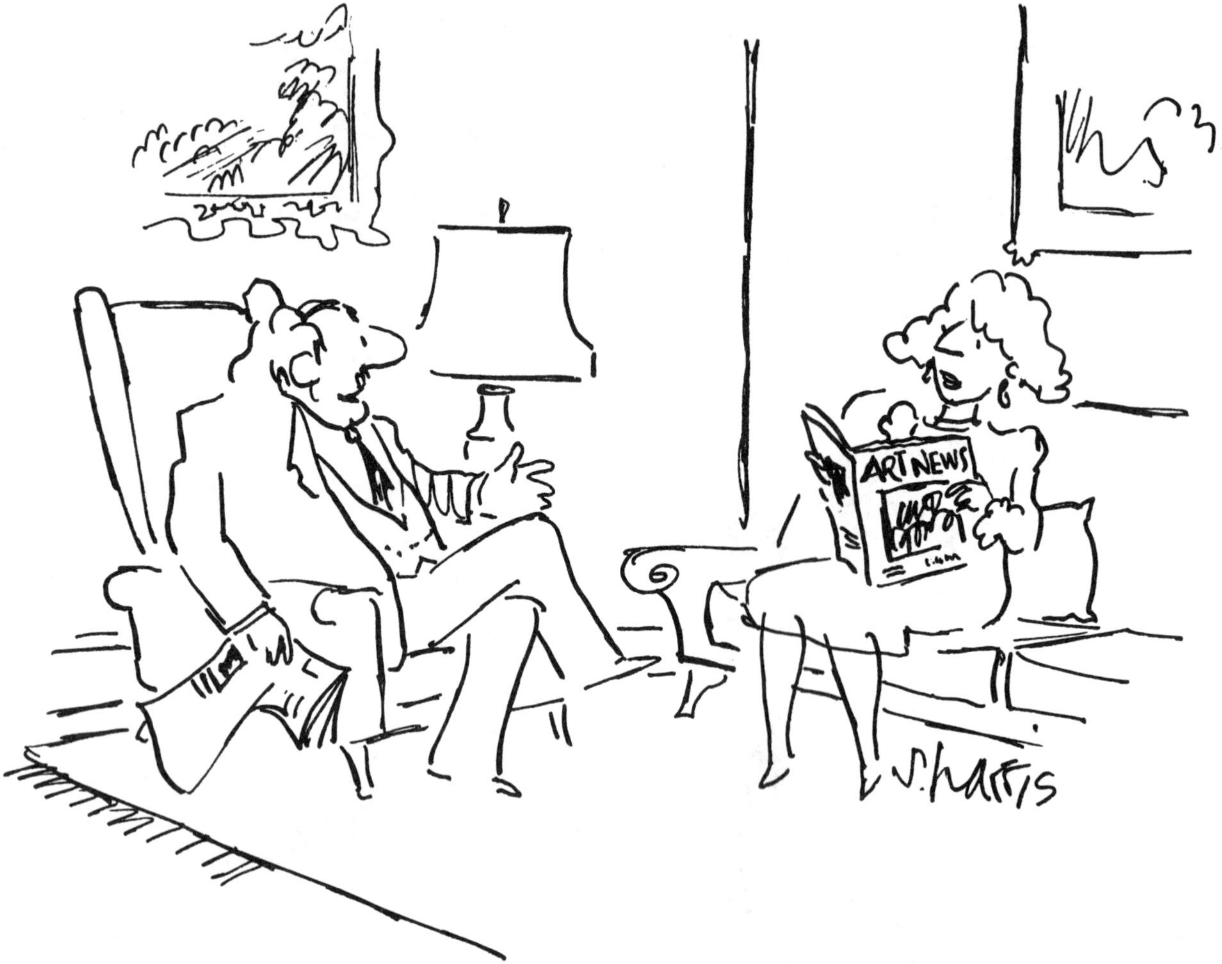
ART NEWS
S. Harris

"Sure I'm interested in symbolism.
Money is a symbol, isn't it?"

SNEDLY & SNEDLY, THE FIRST COMPANY TO LEAVE THE CITY, AND TAKE THEIR BUILDING WITH THEM

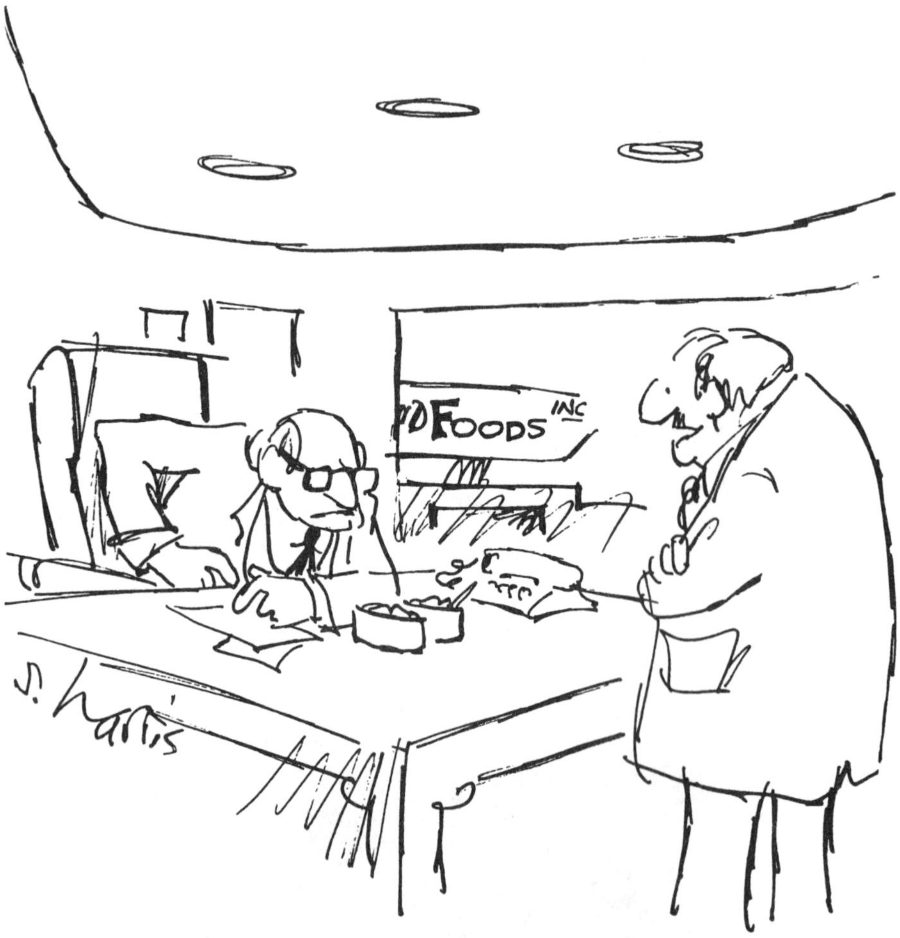
FOODS INC
S. Harris

"Two breakthroughs—imitation eggs made of soybeans and imitation soybeans made of eggs."

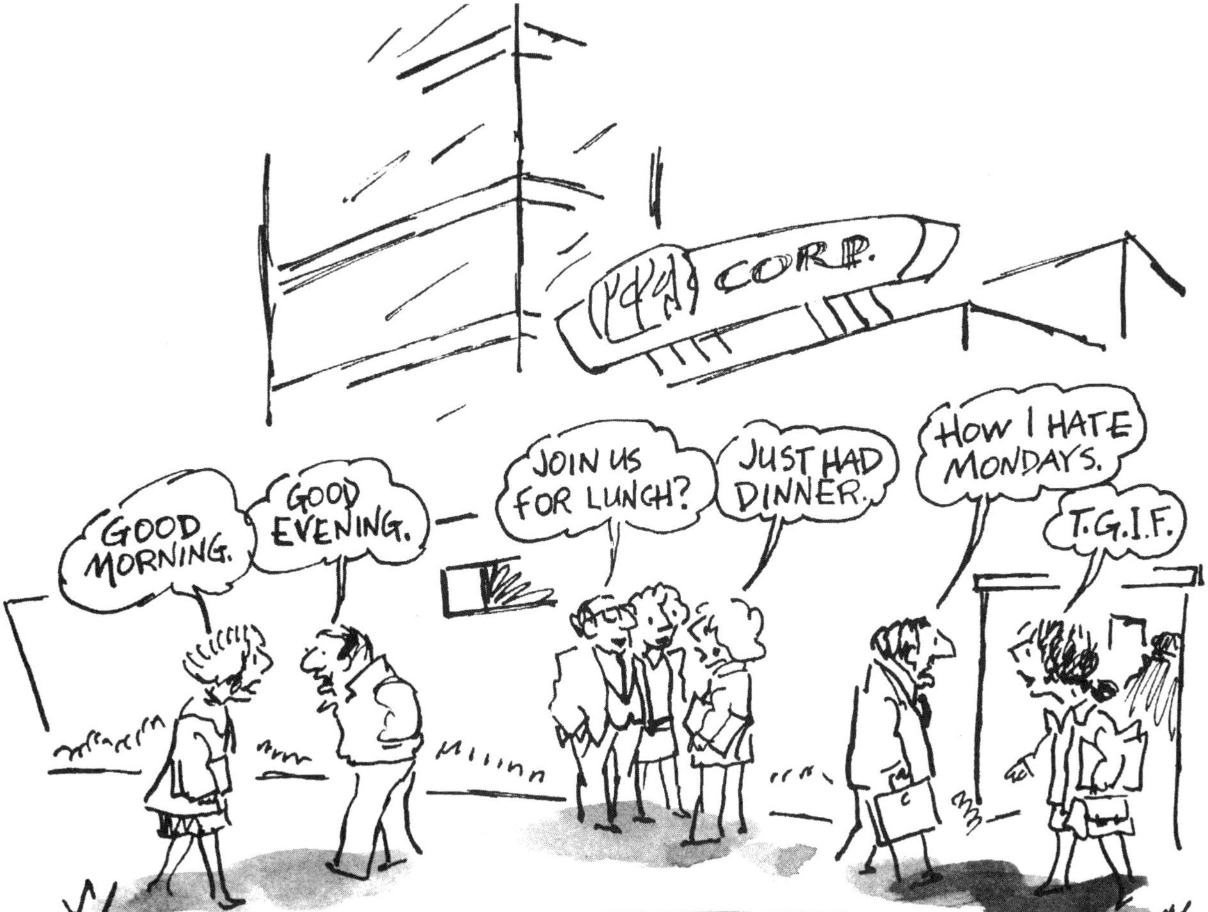
CORP.
GOOD MORNING.
GOOD EVENING.
JOIN US FOR LUNCH?
JUST HAD DINNER.
HOW I HATE MONDAYS.
T.G.I.F.

FLEXTIME

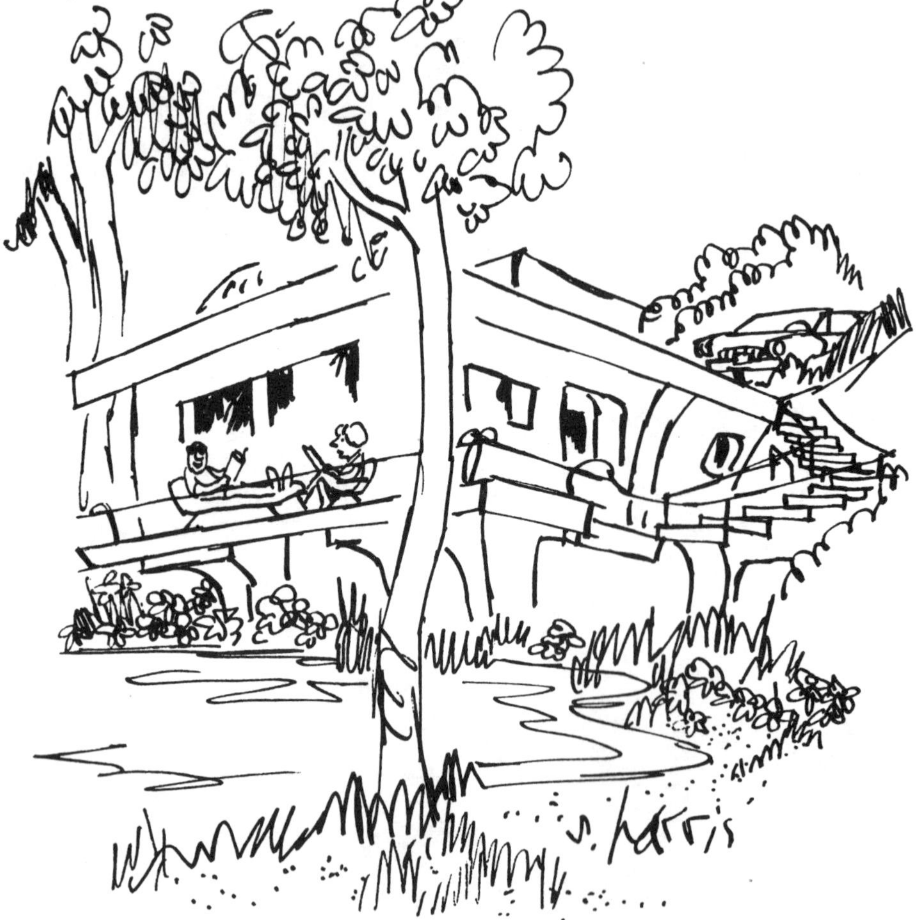
S. Harris

"Yes, sir—Thoreau had the right idea."

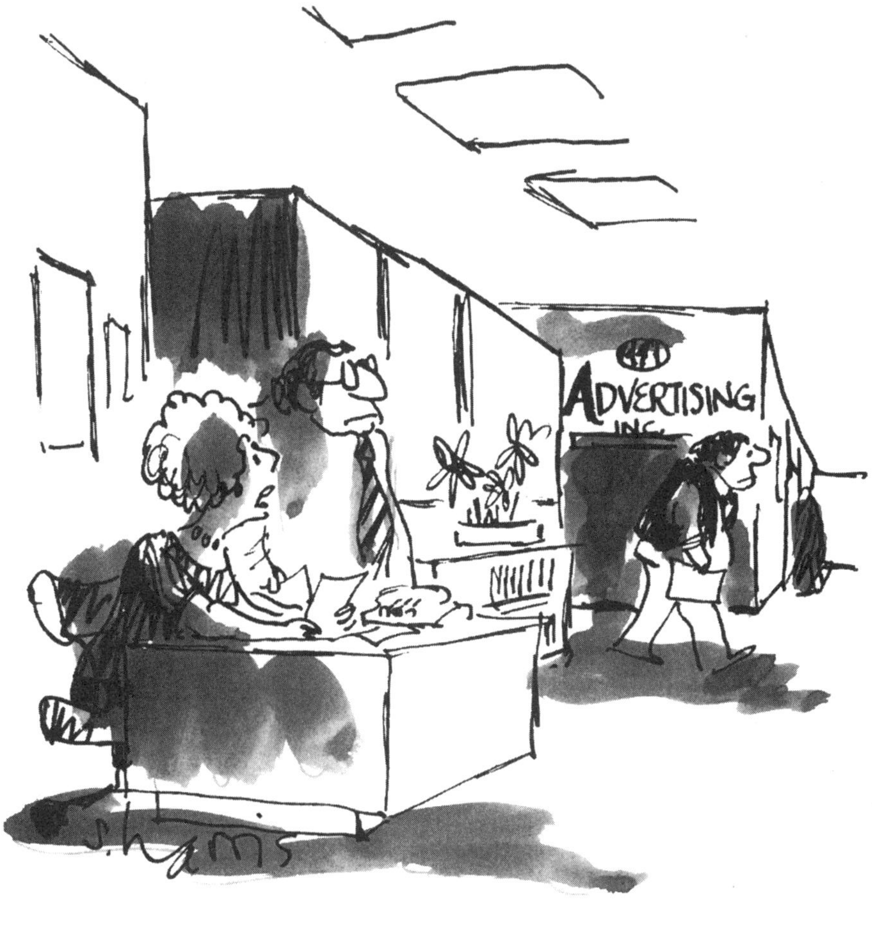
ADVERTISING

"He's written some great slogans and some great labels, but he's never written a great coupon."

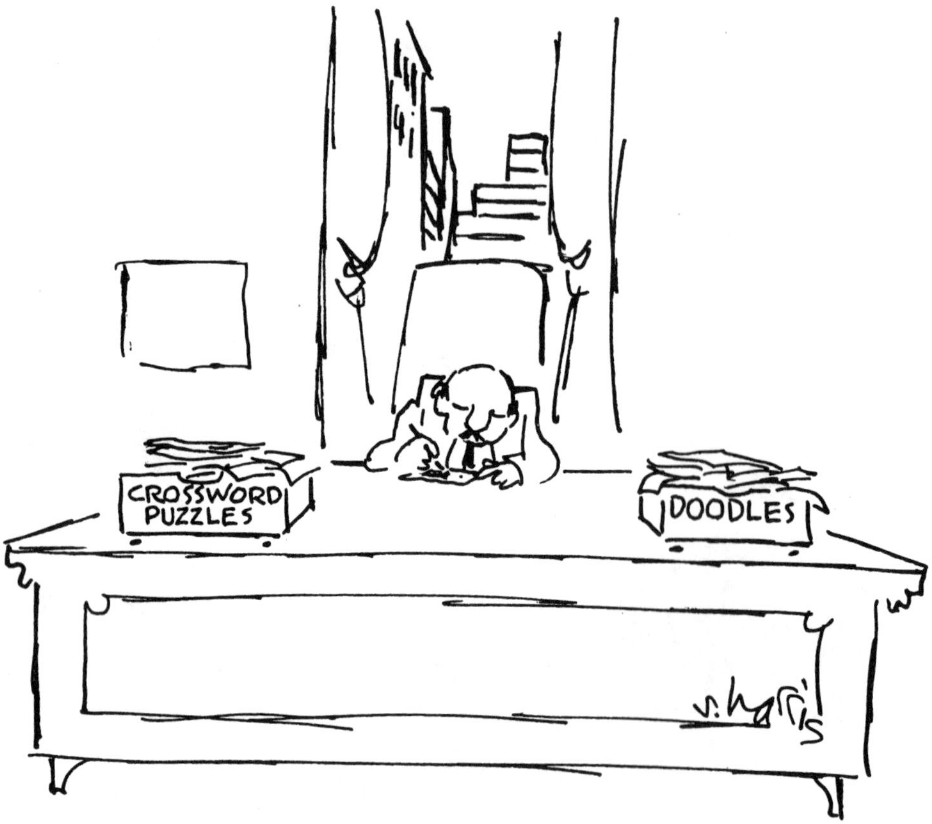
CROSSWORD PUZZLES
DOODLES
v. harris

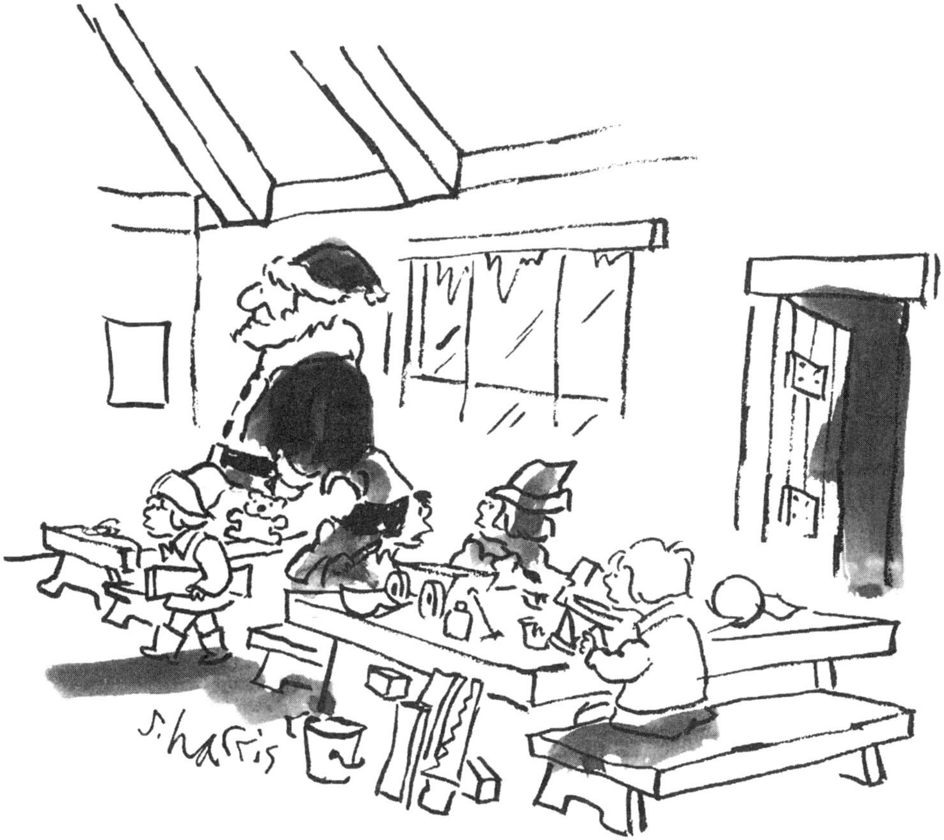
S. harris

"As I understand it, he has a whole other workshop in Hong Kong where they make all that electronic stuff."

"We think of our estimates as merely a quest for the truth."

"*. . . and <u>these</u> are <u>my</u> averages.*"

"I just _sell_ stocks. If you're interested in manipulating them,
you'll have to talk to one of our senior officers."

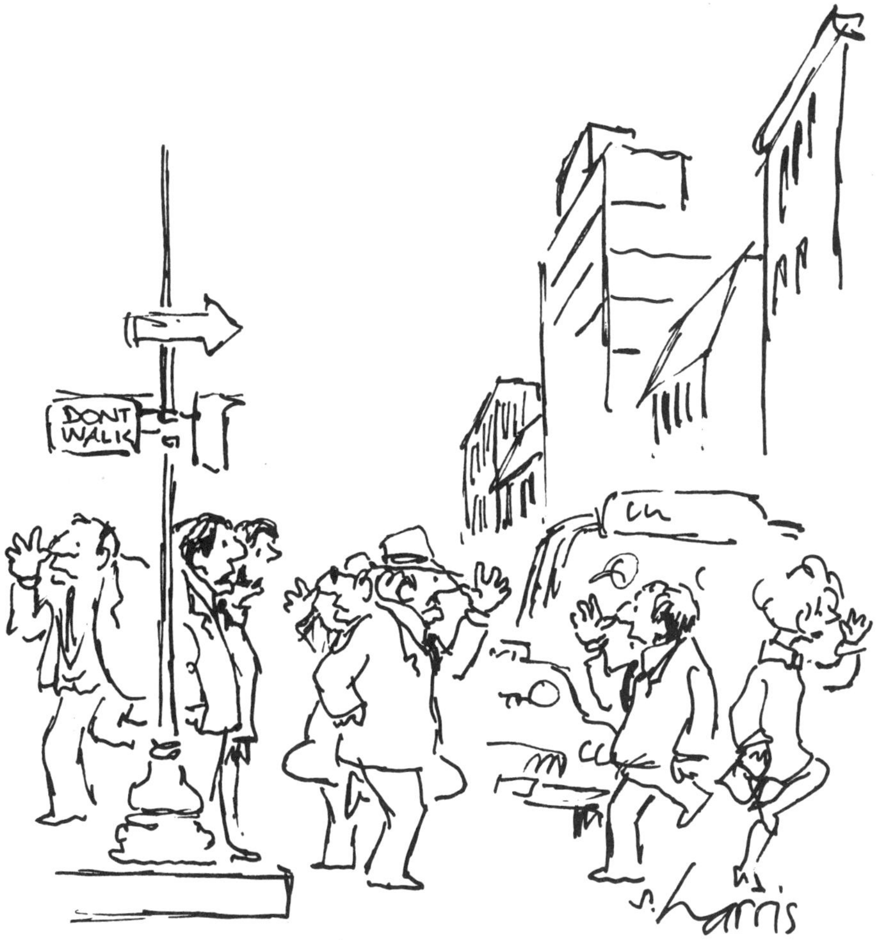
DONT
WALK

"It's either mass hysteria, or a very effective advertising campaign."

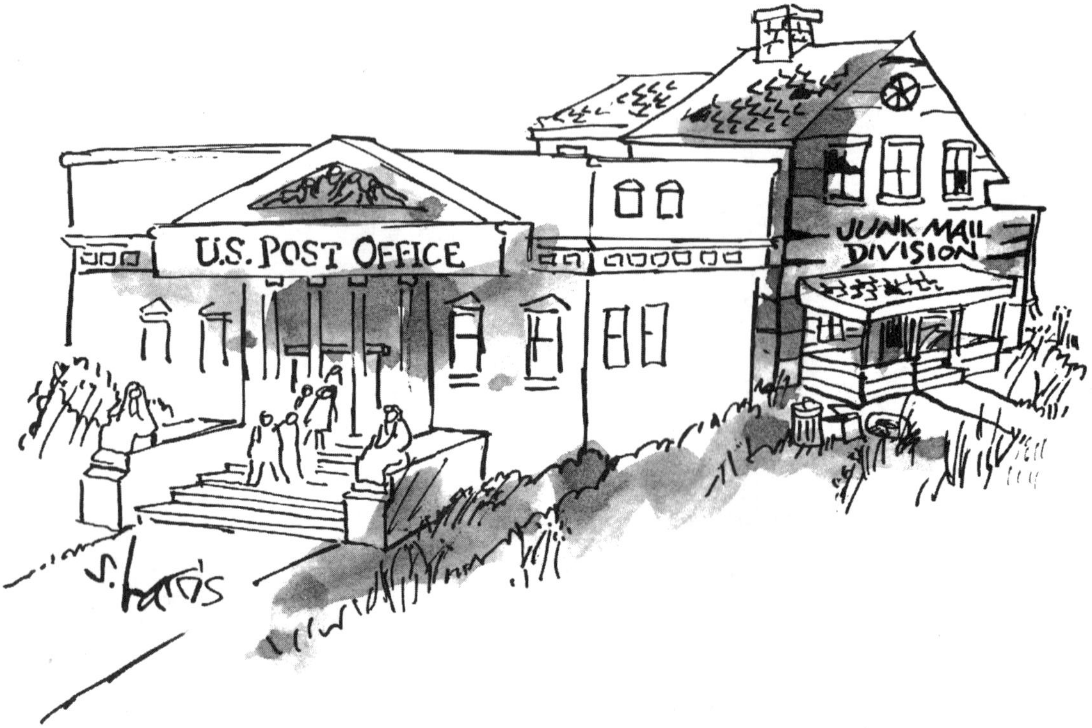
U.S. POST OFFICE
JUNK MAIL DIVISION
S. Harris

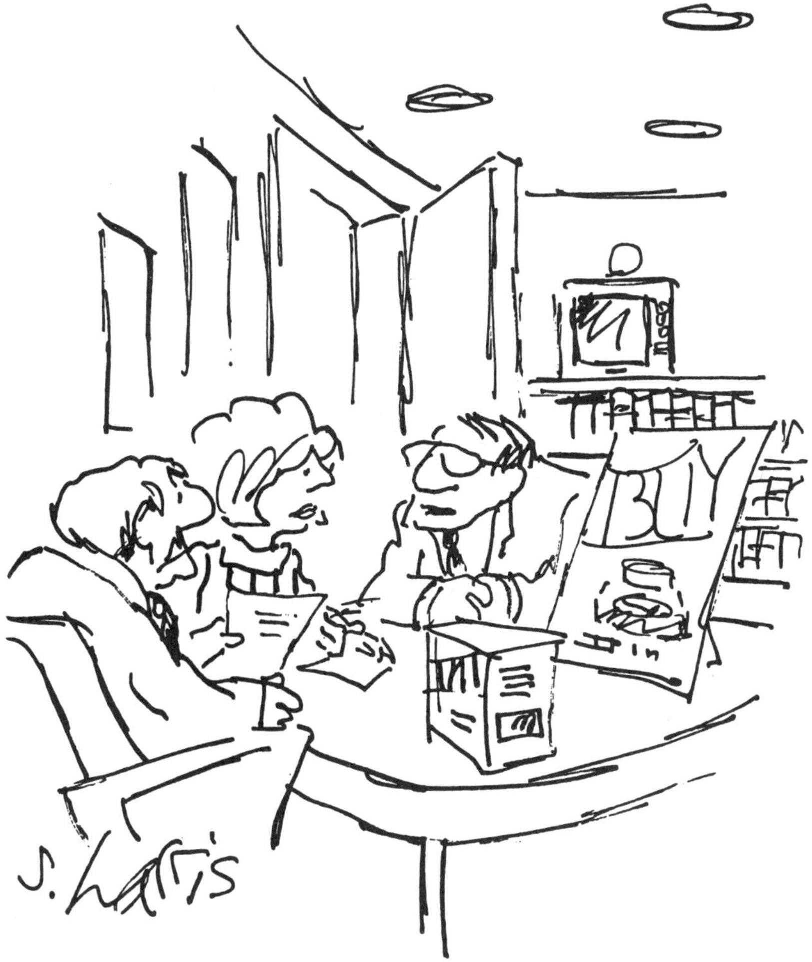
BUY
S. Harris

"It won't bother us if we're not allowed to aim our ads at the kids. The adults are easier to fool anyway."

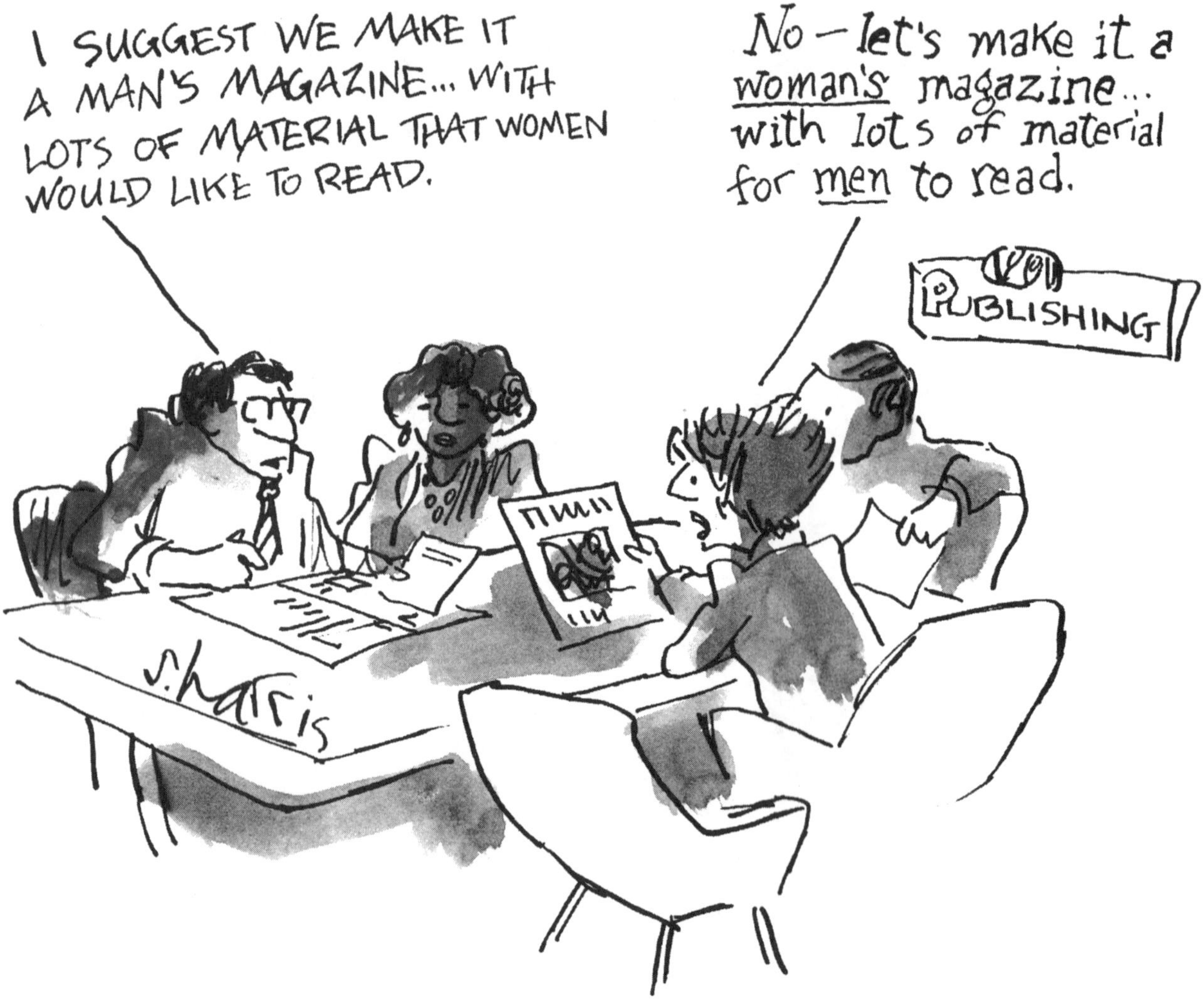
I SUGGEST WE MAKE IT A MAN'S MAGAZINE... WITH LOTS OF MATERIAL THAT WOMEN WOULD LIKE TO READ.
No – let's make it a woman's magazine... with lots of material for men to read.
PUBLISHING
S. Harris

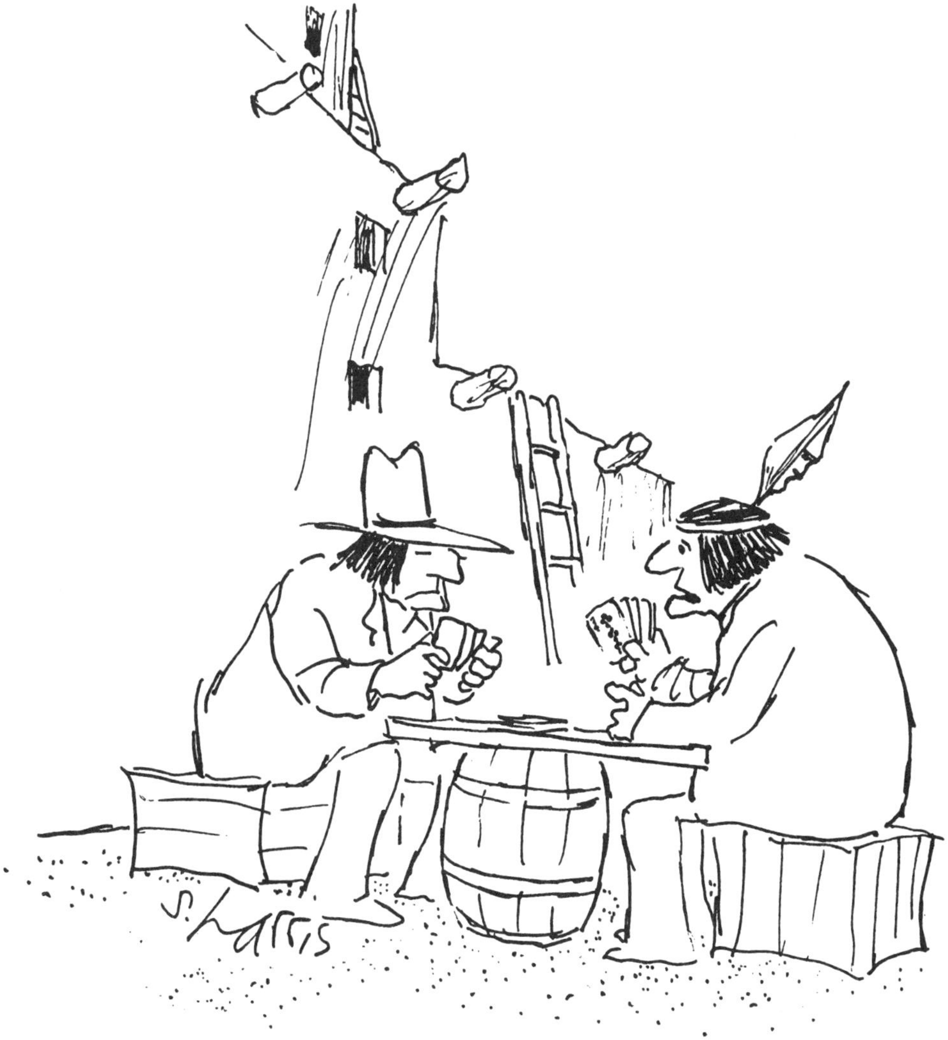
S. Harris

"I'll see your 10,000 Arizona acres ripe for development and I'll raise you 10,000 acres of glorious mountain hideaways in New Mexico."

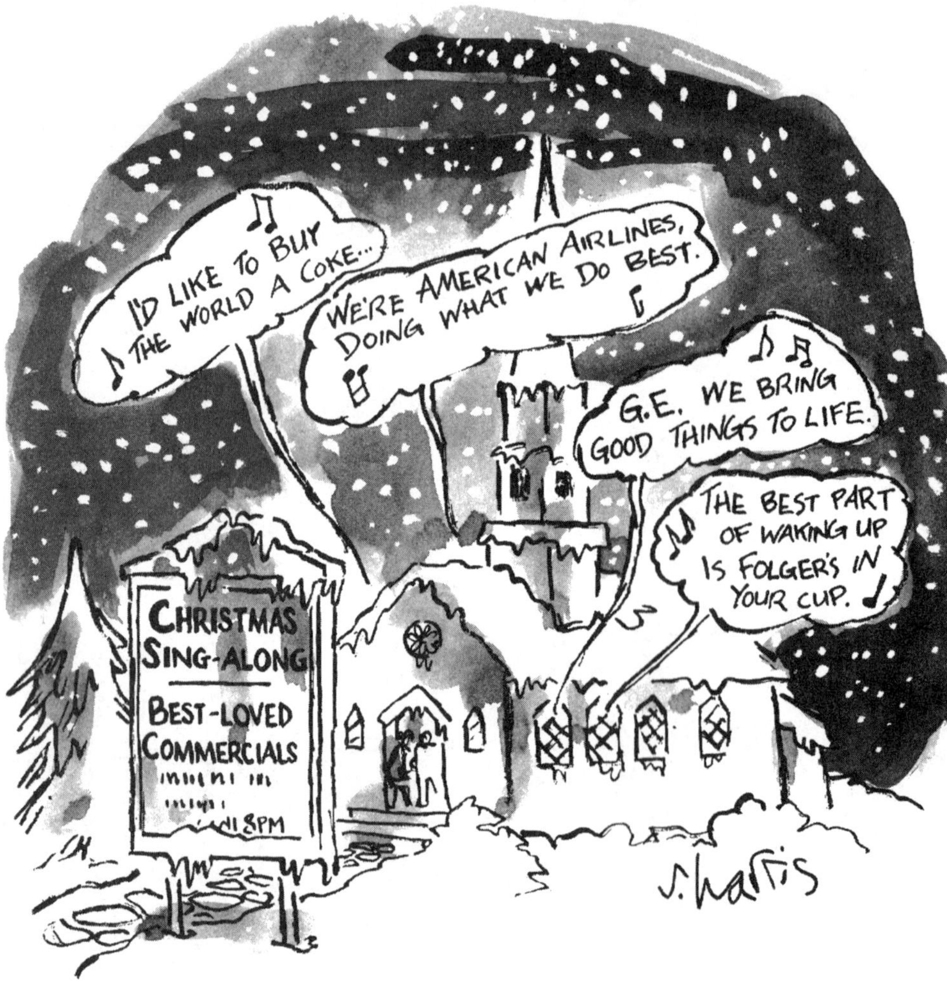
I'D LIKE TO BUY THE WORLD A COKE...
WE'RE AMERICAN AIRLINES, DOING WHAT WE DO BEST.
G.E. WE BRING GOOD THINGS TO LIFE.
THE BEST PART OF WAKING UP IS FOLGER'S IN YOUR CUP.
CHRISTMAS SING-ALONG
BEST-LOVED COMMERCIALS
S. Harris

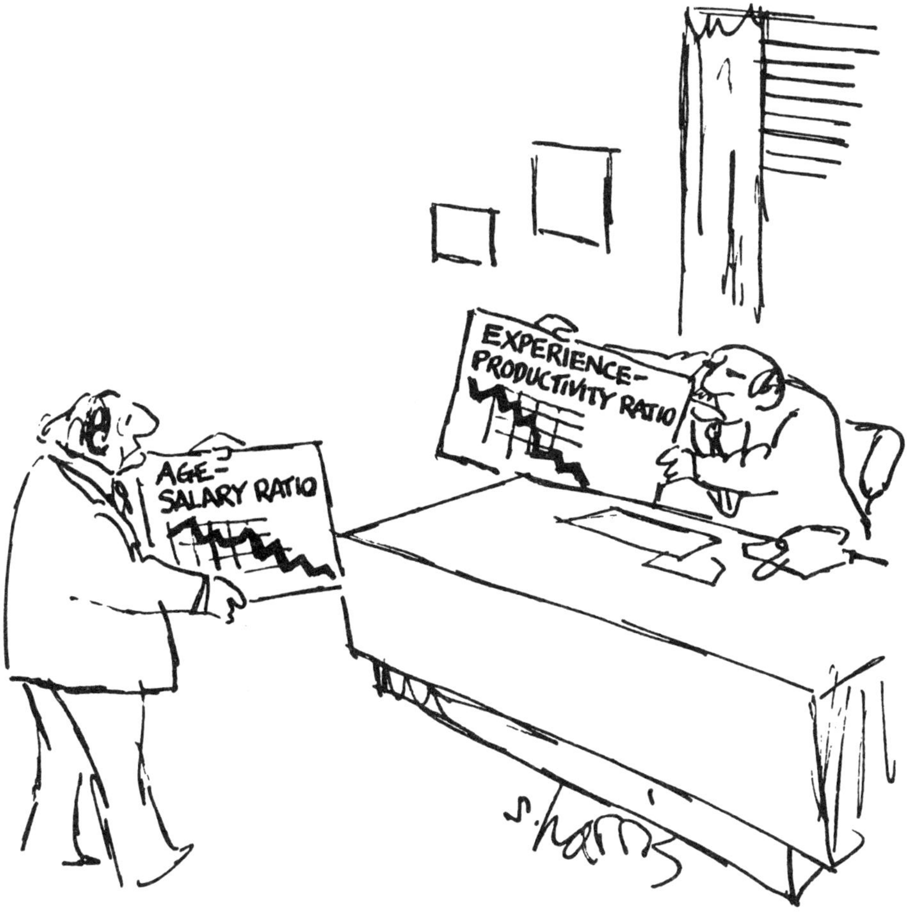

AGE-
SALARY RATIO
EXPERIENCE-
PRODUCTIVITY RATIO
S. Harris

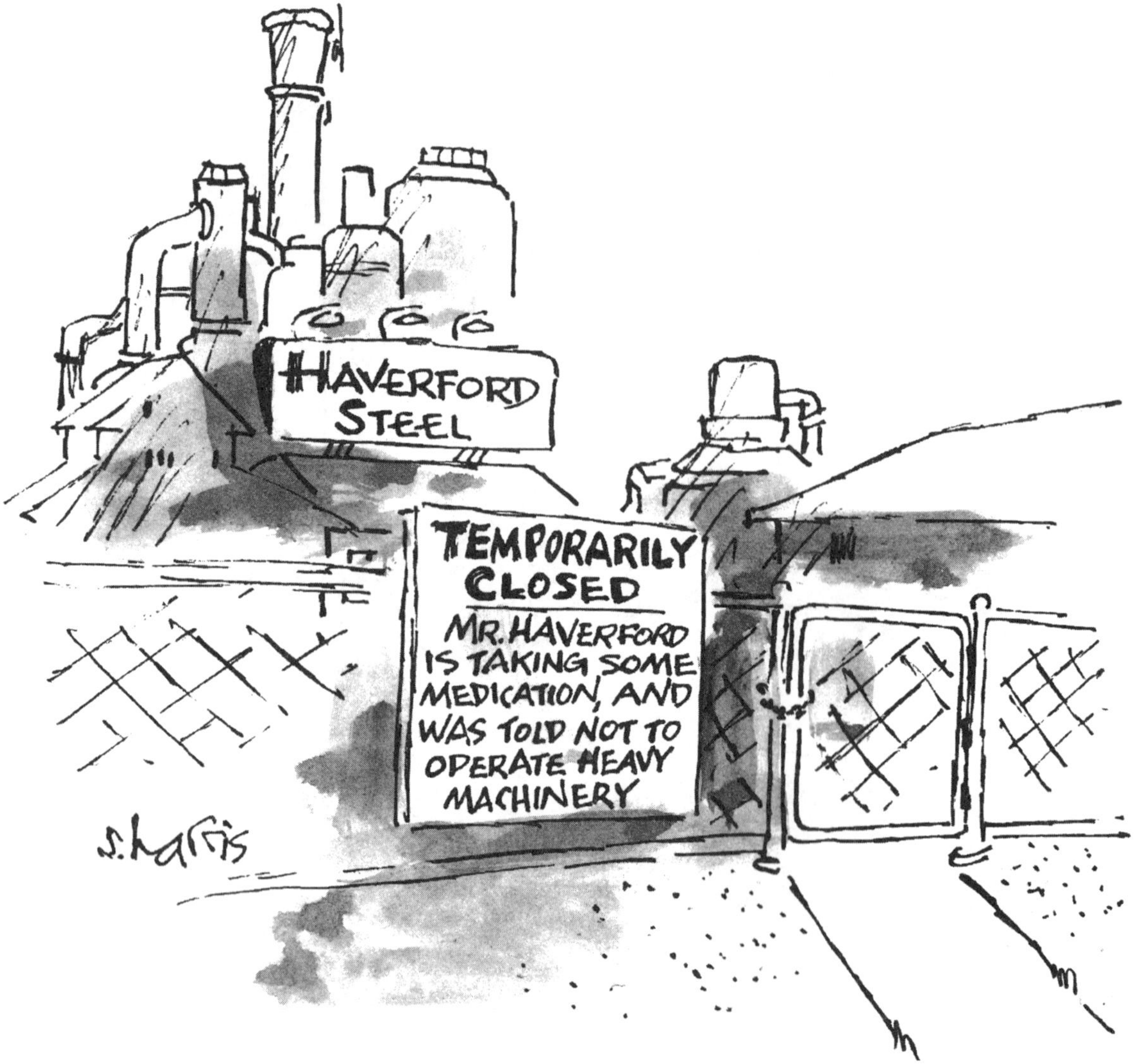
HAVERFORD STEEL
TEMPORARILY CLOSED
MR. HAVERFORD IS TAKING SOME MEDICATION, AND WAS TOLD NOT TO OPERATE HEAVY MACHINERY
S. harris

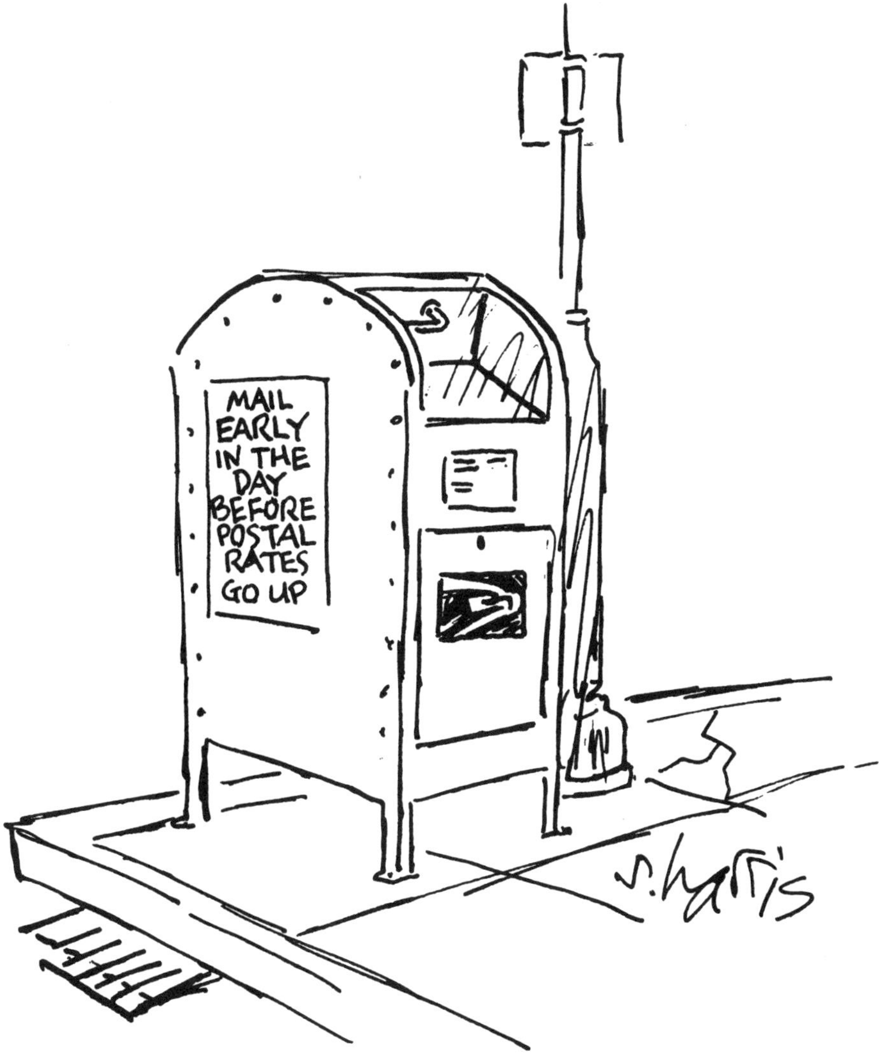
MAIL EARLY IN THE DAY BEFORE POSTAL RATES GO UP
S. Harris

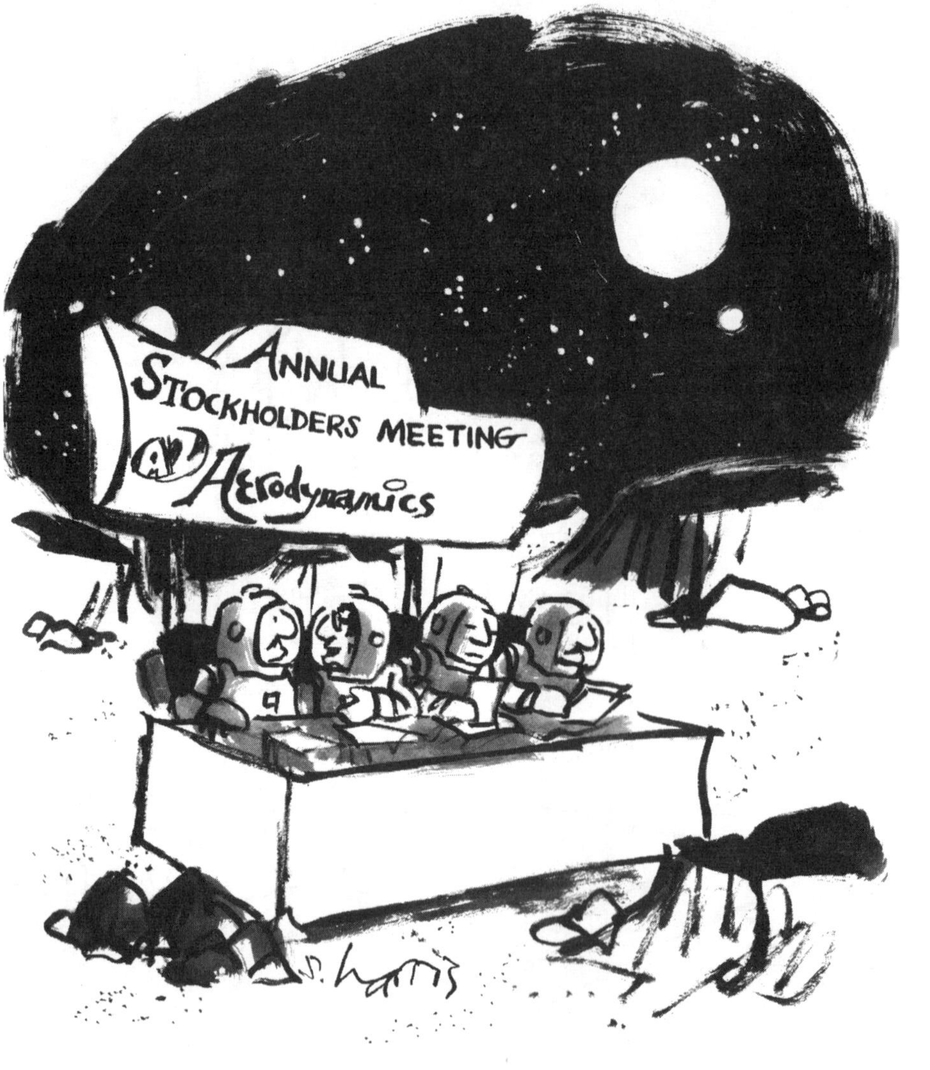
ANNUAL
STOCKHOLDERS MEETING
AM
AErodynamics
S. Harris

"We did our part. If they didn't show up, that's their business."

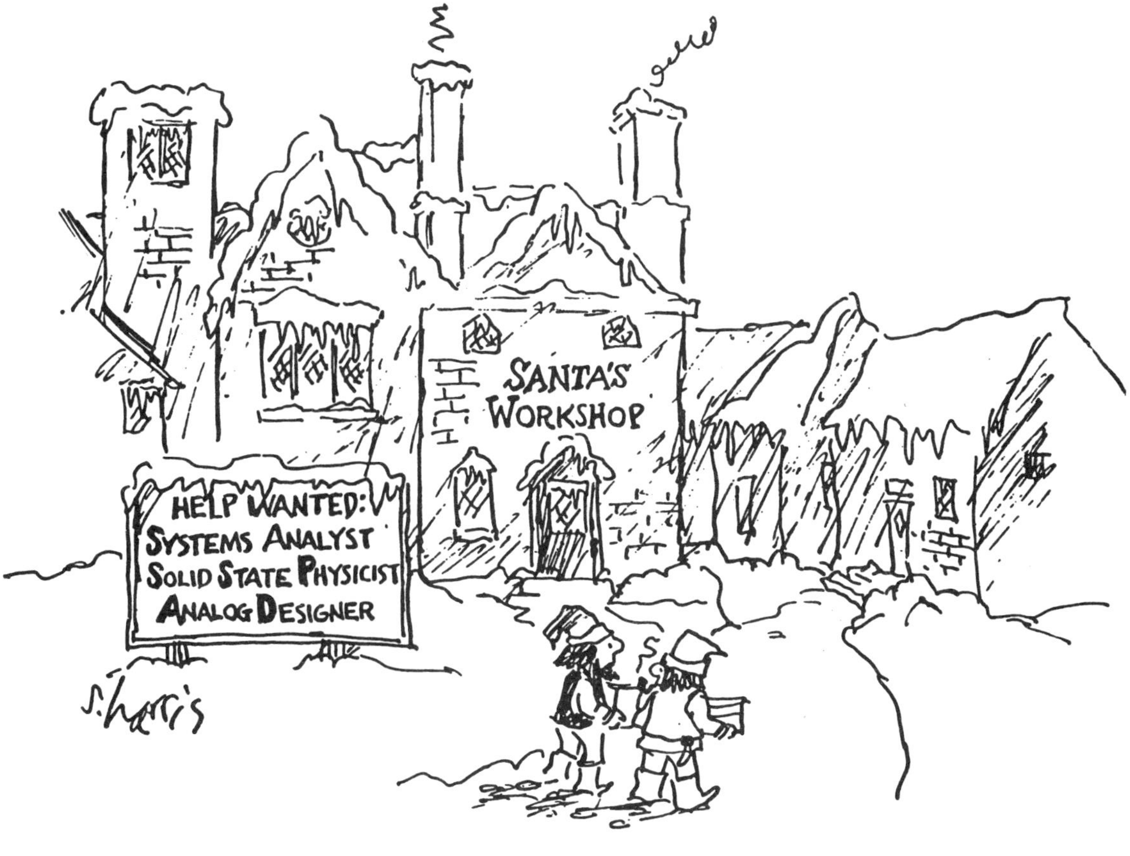
SANTA'S WORKSHOP
HELP WANTED:
SYSTEMS ANALYST
SOLID STATE PHYSICIST
ANALOG DESIGNER
S. Harris

"I can remember when all we needed was someone who could carve and someone who could sew."

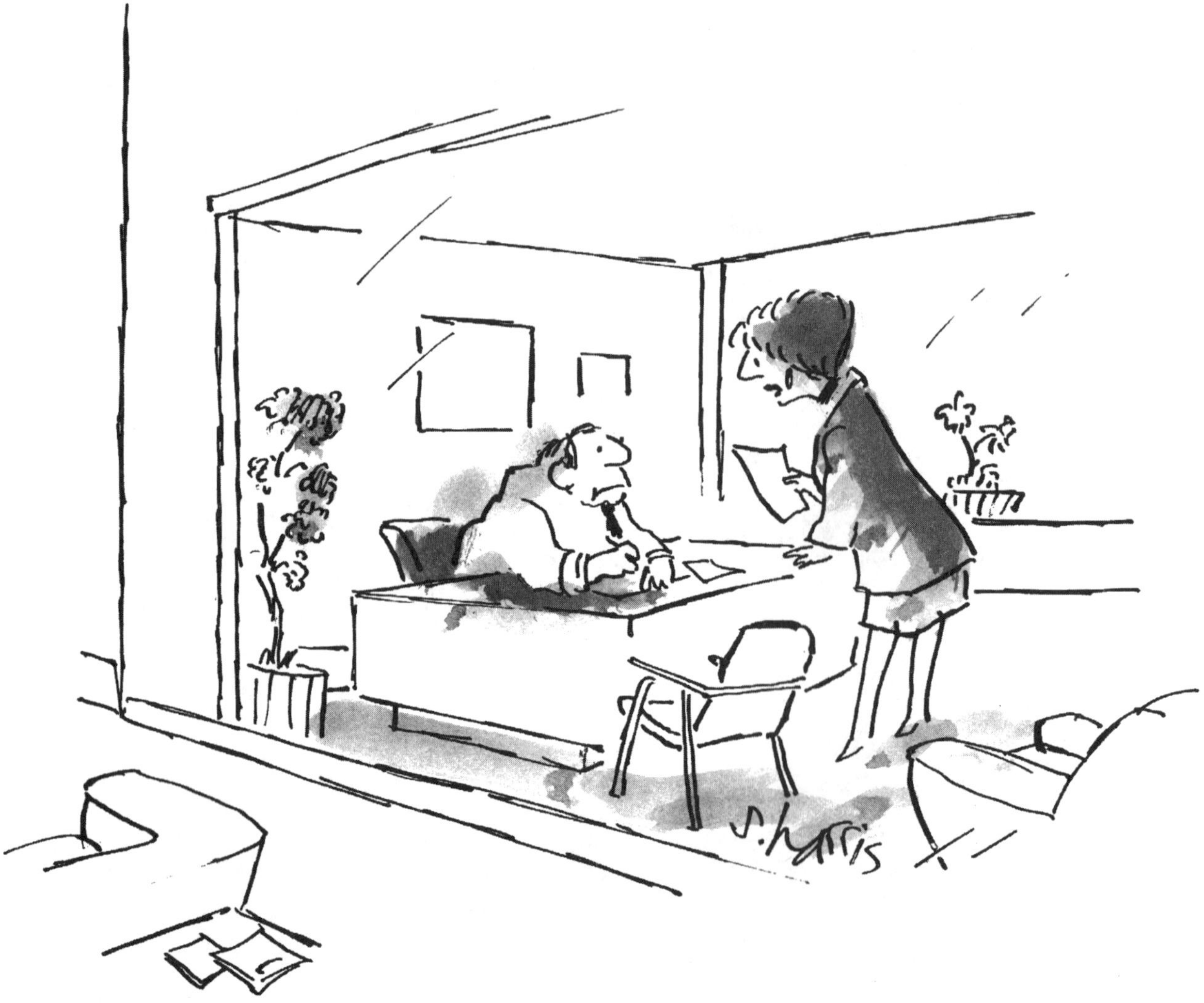
S.Harris

"It's worse than we thought—there's going to be random testing for competence."

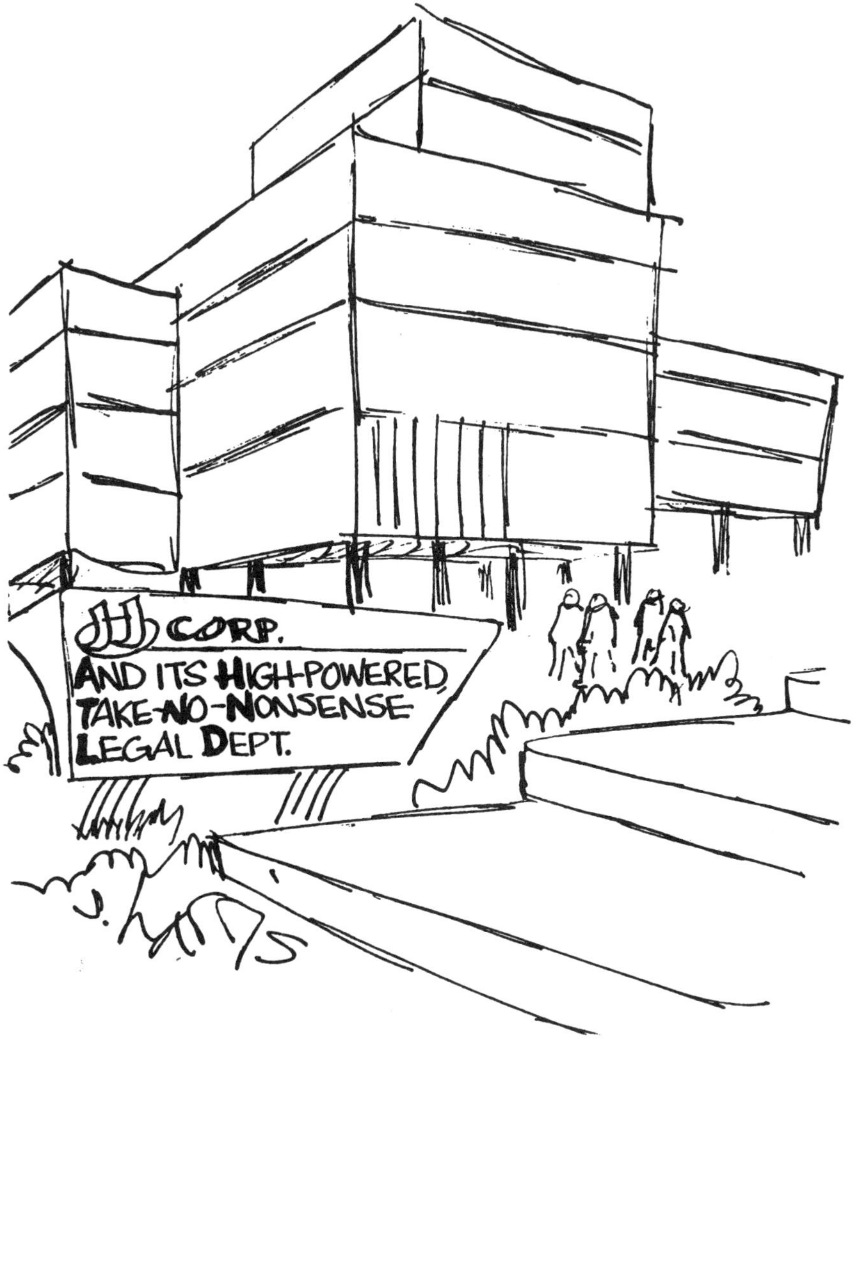
CORP.
AND ITS HIGH-POWERED,
TAKE-NO-NONSENSE
LEGAL DEPT.

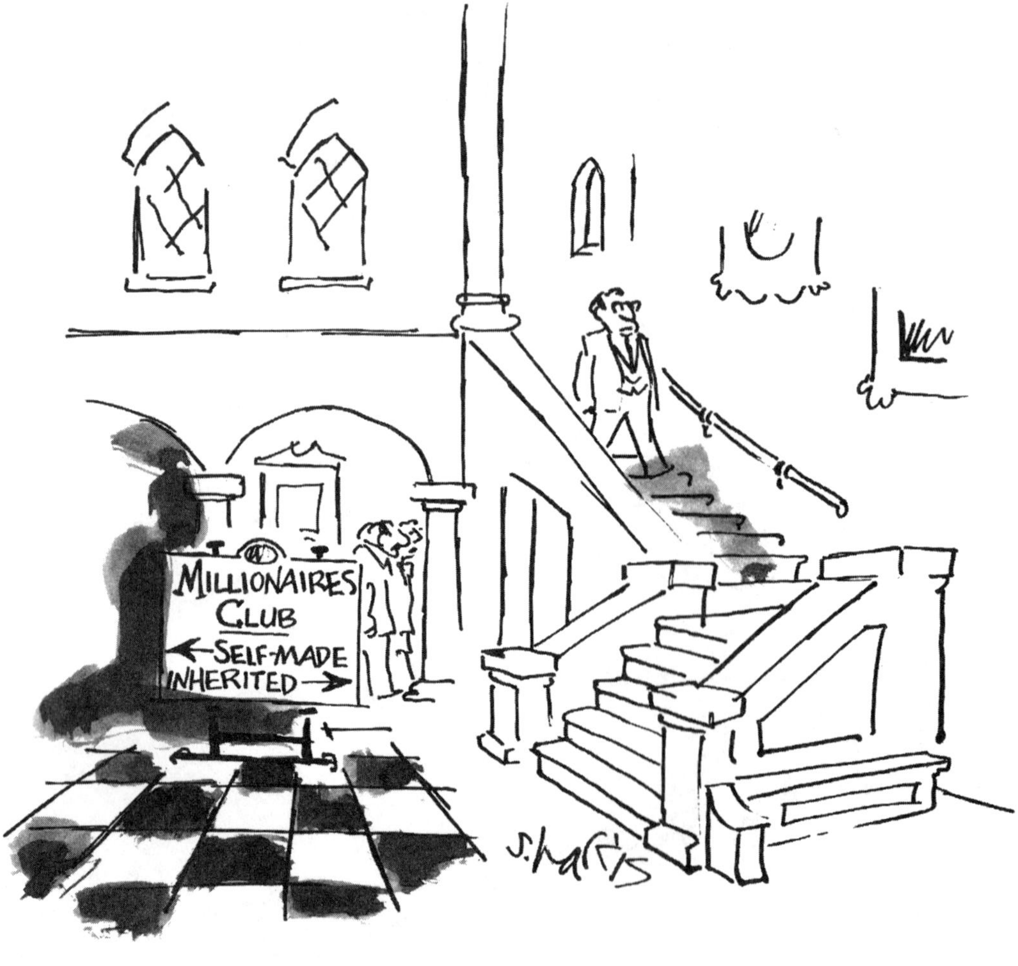
MILLIONAIRES
CLUB
←SELF-MADE
INHERITED→
S.Harris

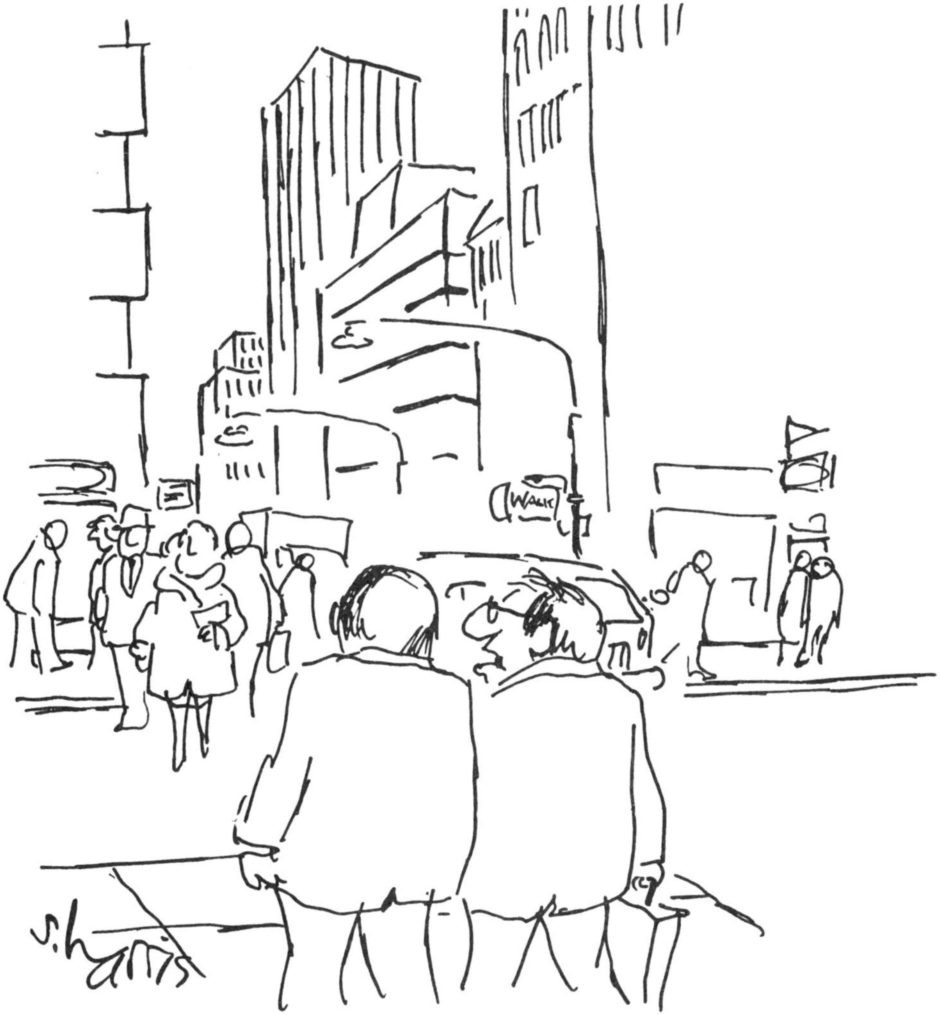
WALK
S.harris

*"At every corner I face the same questions:
Should I go forward? Should I go to the left?
Should I go to the right? Where does my fortune lie?"*

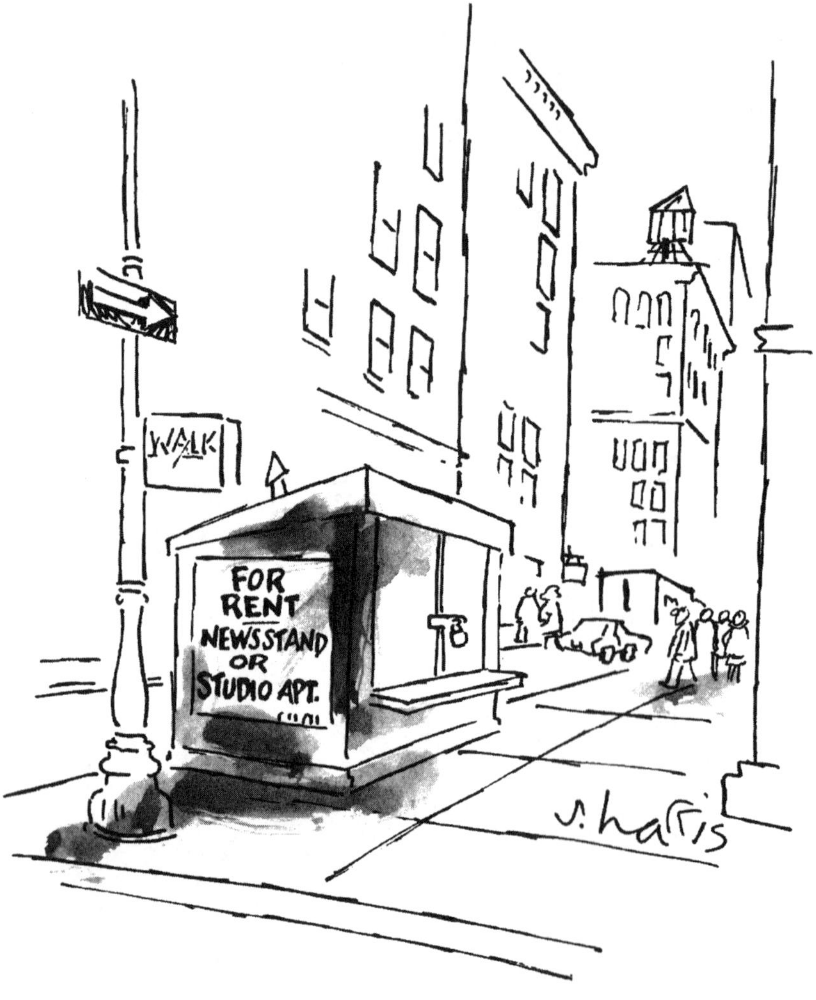
WALK
FOR RENT
NEWSSTAND OR STUDIO APT.
S. harris

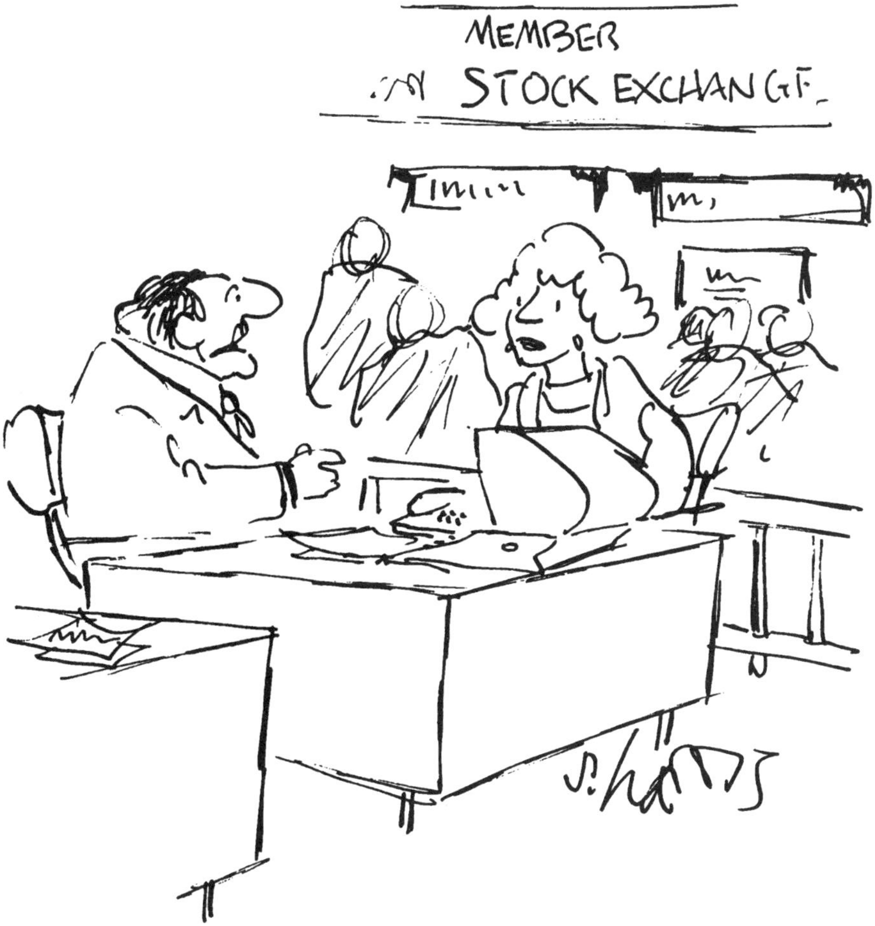
MEMBER
STOCK EXCHANGE

"We have an excellent investment counselor and if things don't work out, an equally good investment therapist."

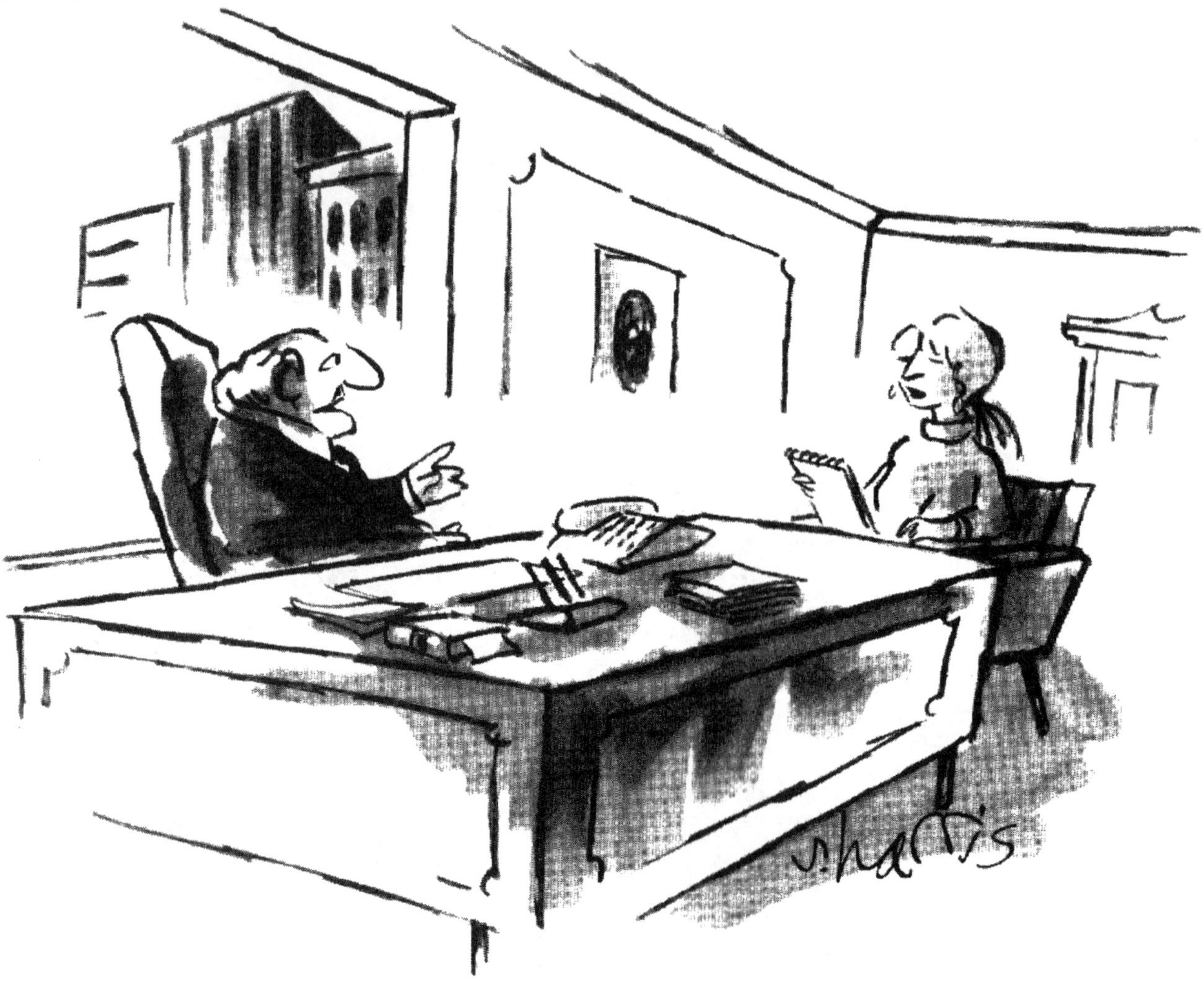

"Type that up, make ten thousand copies, and send them to all the important people in the world."

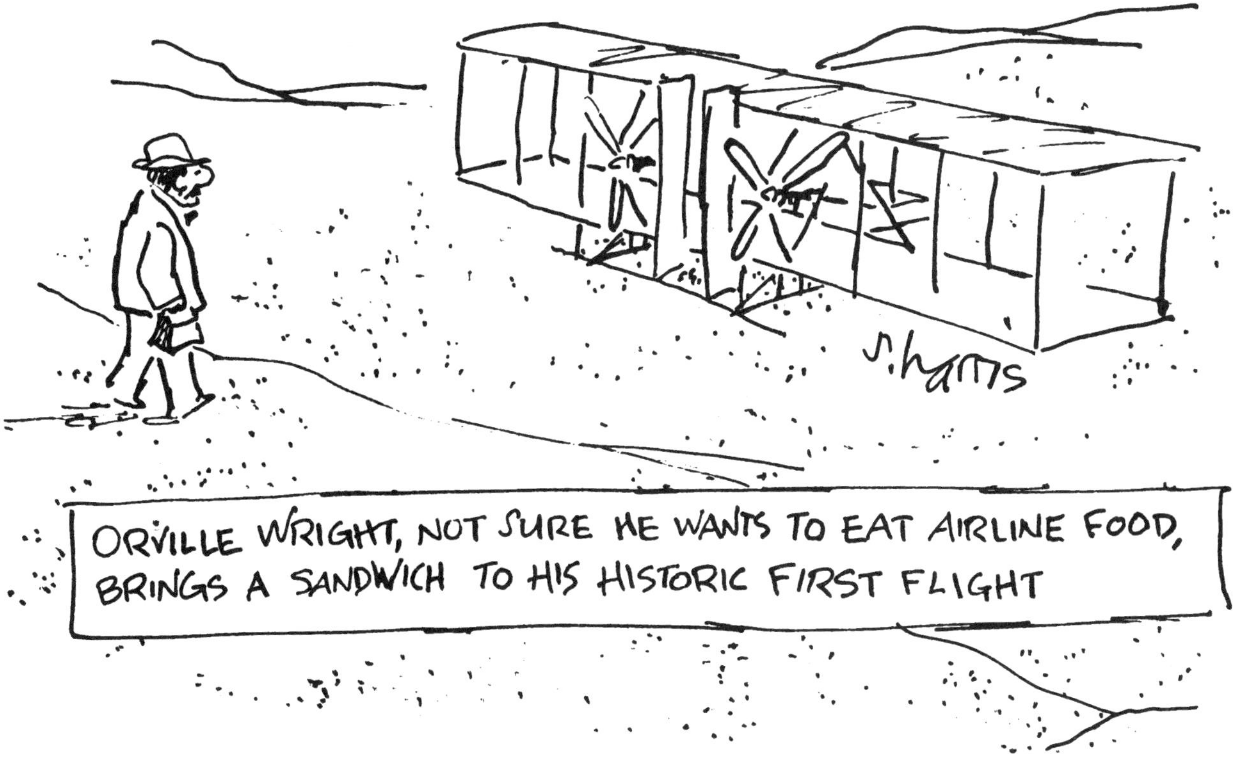
S. harris

ORVILLE WRIGHT, NOT SURE HE WANTS TO EAT AIRLINE FOOD, BRINGS A SANDWICH TO HIS HISTORIC FIRST FLIGHT

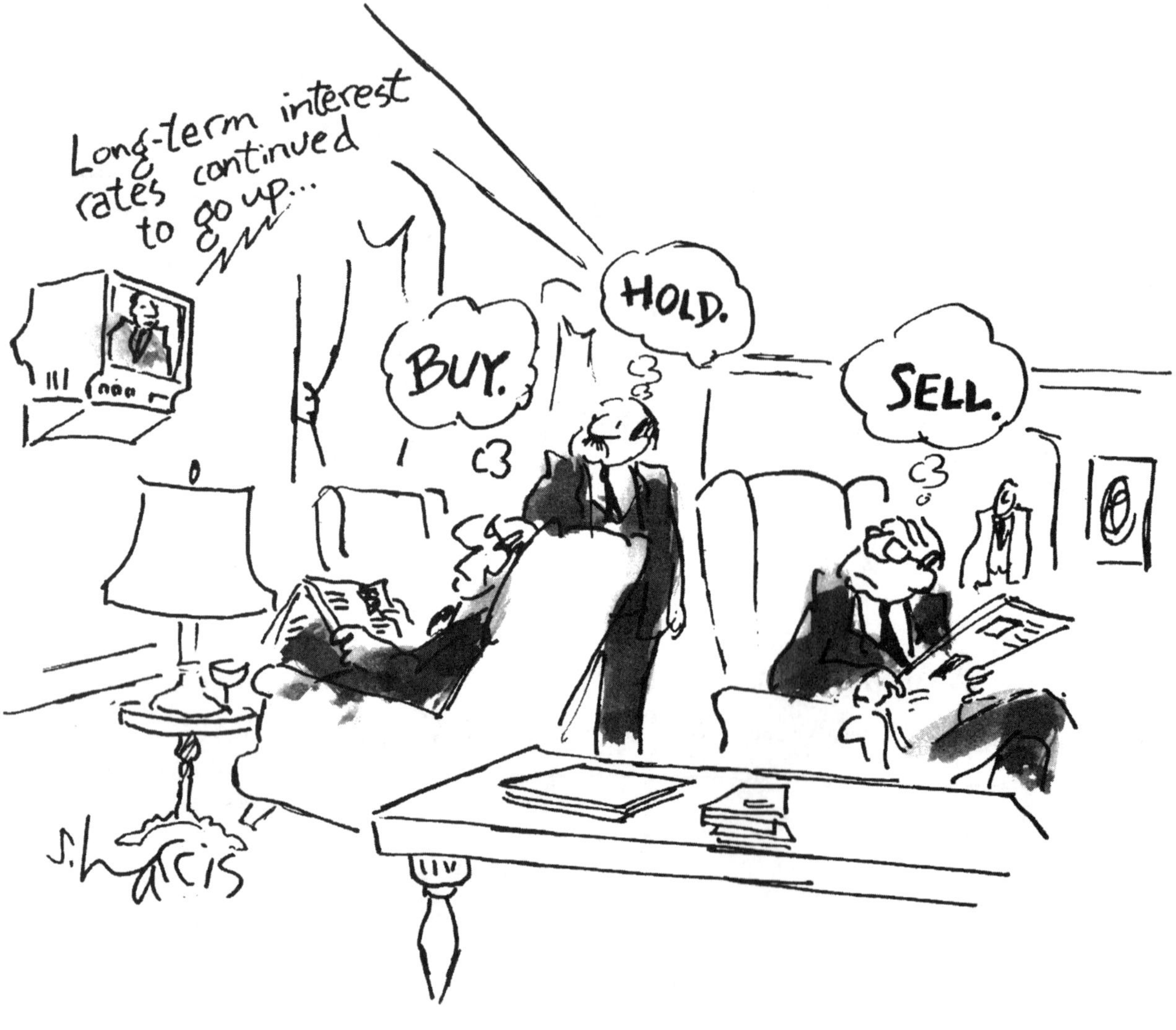
Long-term interest rates continued to go up...
BUY.
HOLD.
SELL.
S. Harris

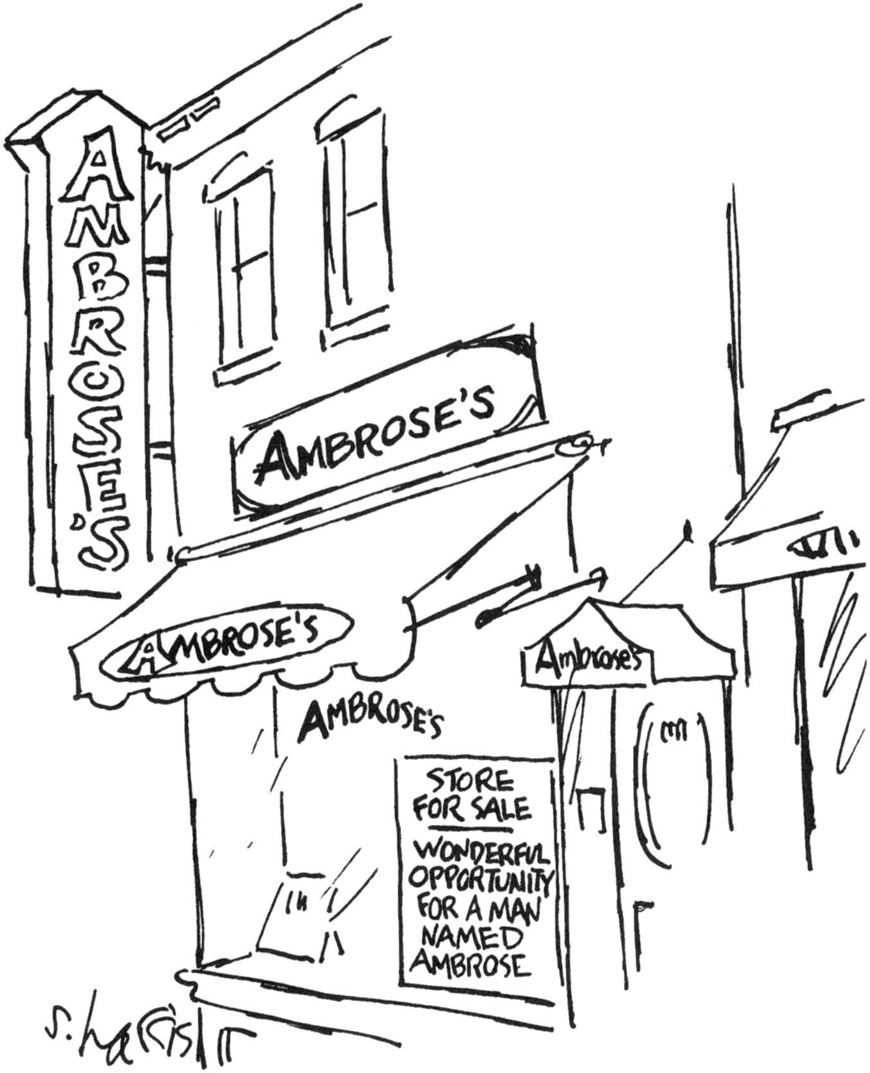
AMBROSE'S
AMBROSE'S
AMBROSE'S
Ambrose's
AMBROSE'S
STORE FOR SALE
WONDERFUL OPPORTUNITY FOR A MAN NAMED AMBROSE

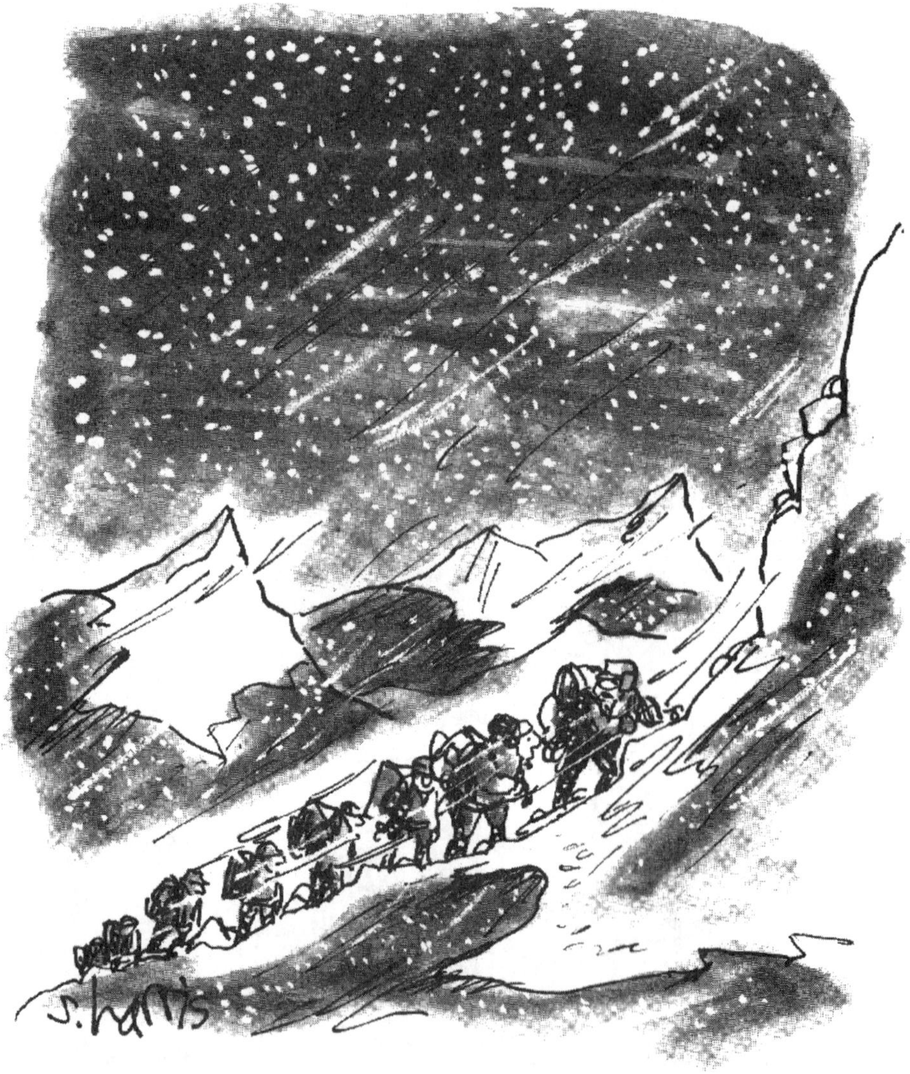
S. harris

"No wonder prices are slightly higher north of the Himalayas."

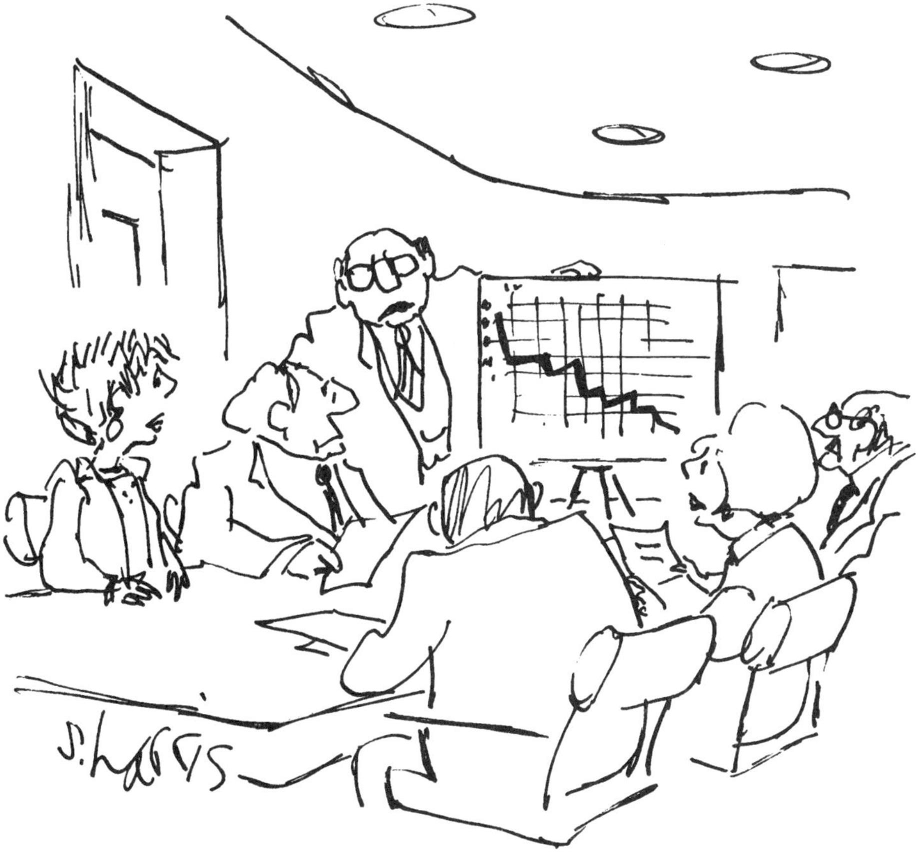
S. Harris

"It isn't that we don't have any high technology.
We don't have any technology."

"We have no quorum, Ms. Hedgely. _I'm_ here, and that's all that matters."

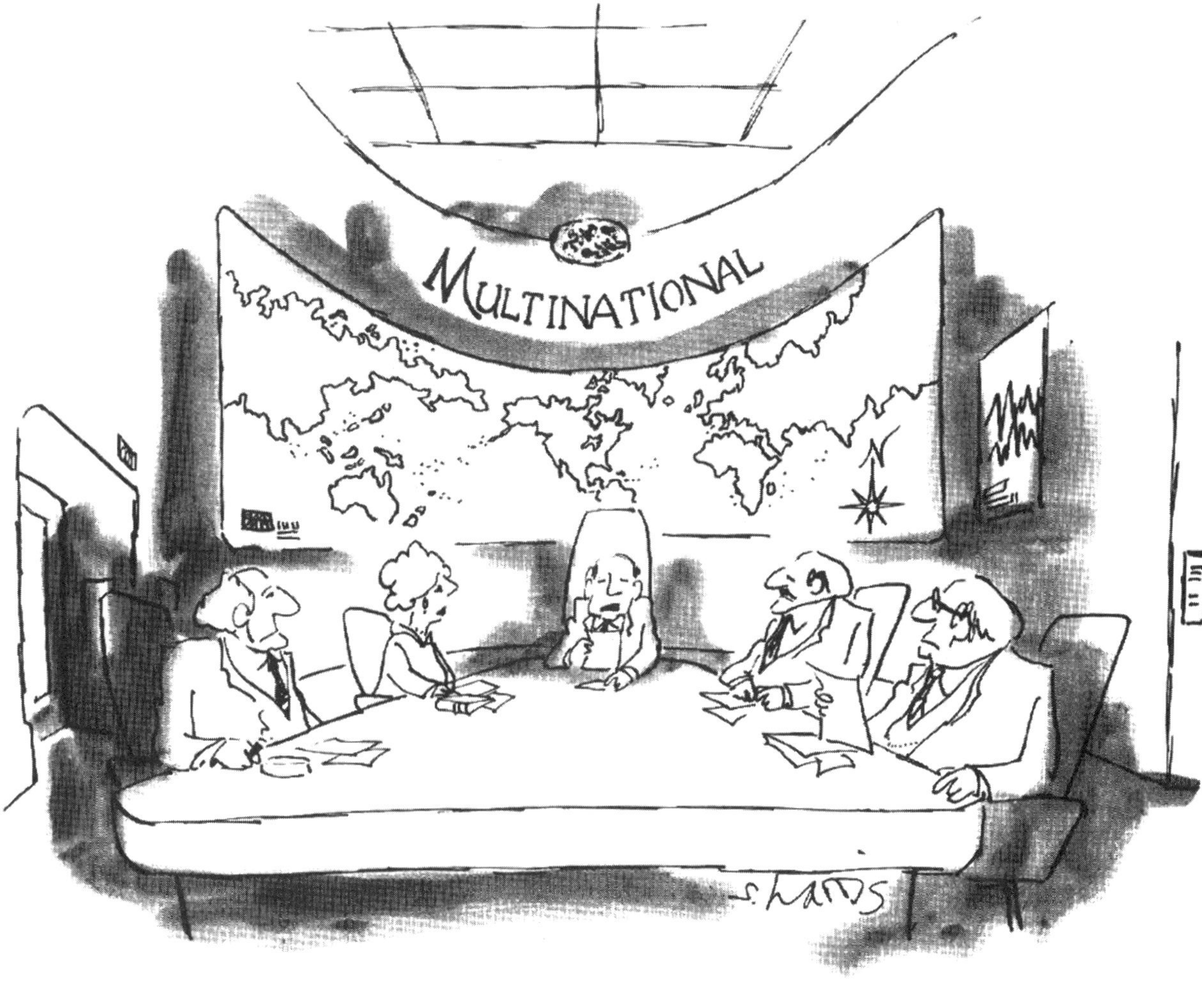
MULTINATIONAL

"It doesn't look good. Some of our nationals are at war with some of our other nationals."

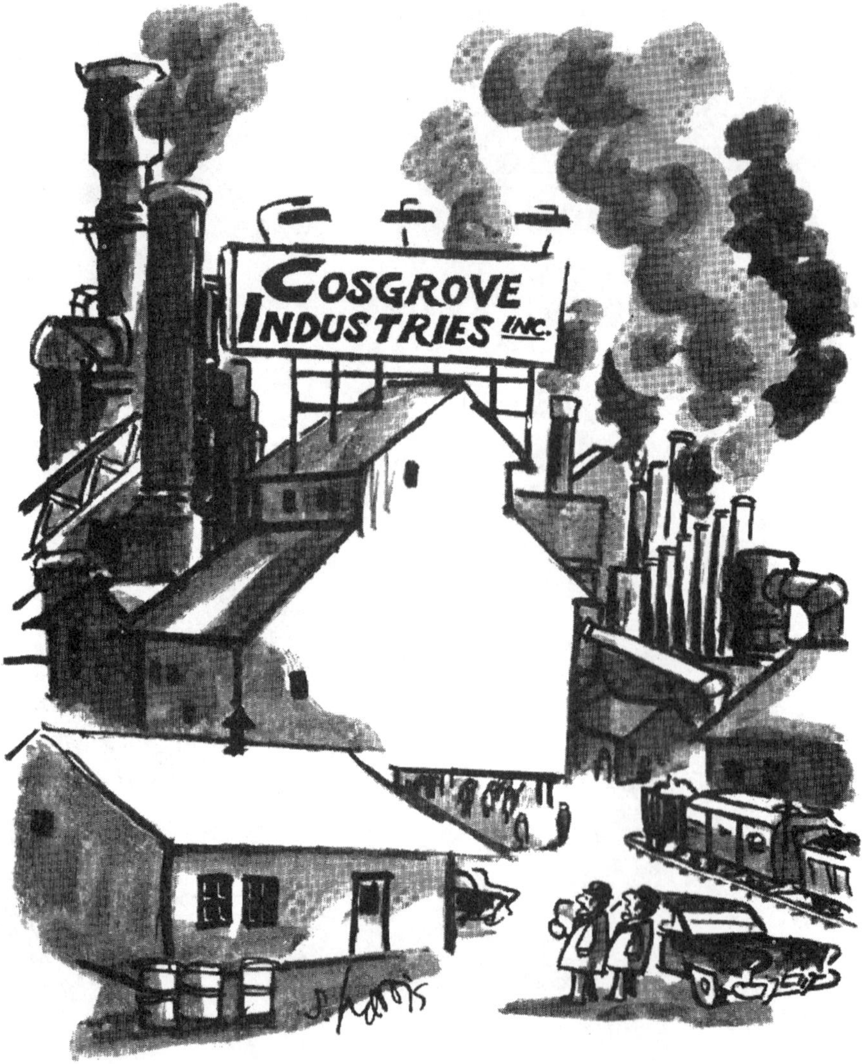
COSGROVE
INDUSTRIES INC.

"Is this another one of your get-rich-quick schemes, Cosgrove?"

"It's on-line, subscribers pay only for the articles they want, it's updated everyday—are you <u>sure</u> we can call it a <u>magazine</u>?"

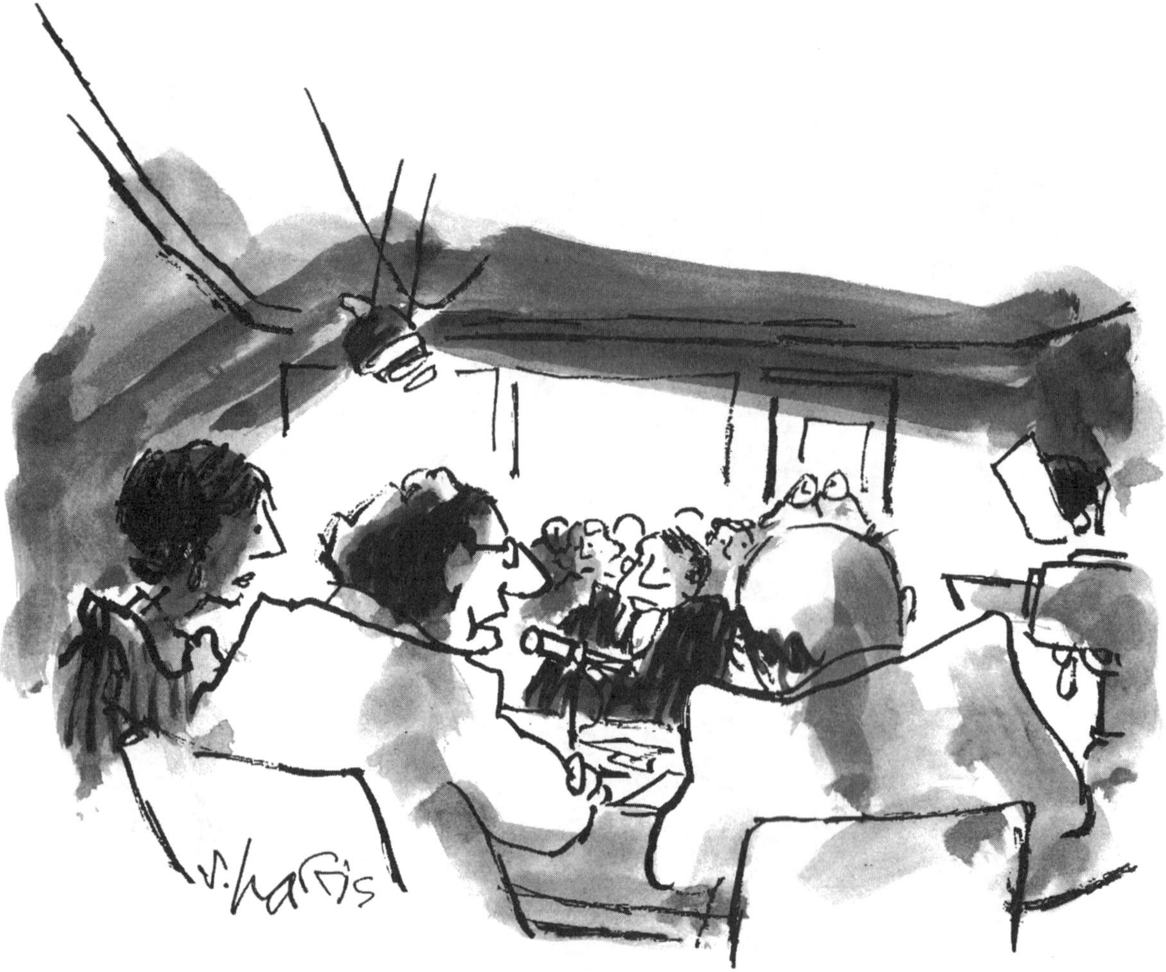
S. Harris

"If you must know, Mr. Davis, we're investigating the baseball card business because the savings and loan mess is too complicated for us."

"*If, for any reason, you are dissatisfied with 'Bryte' soap flakes, send the unused portion back to us, because, frankly, we hate to see any of it go to waste.*"

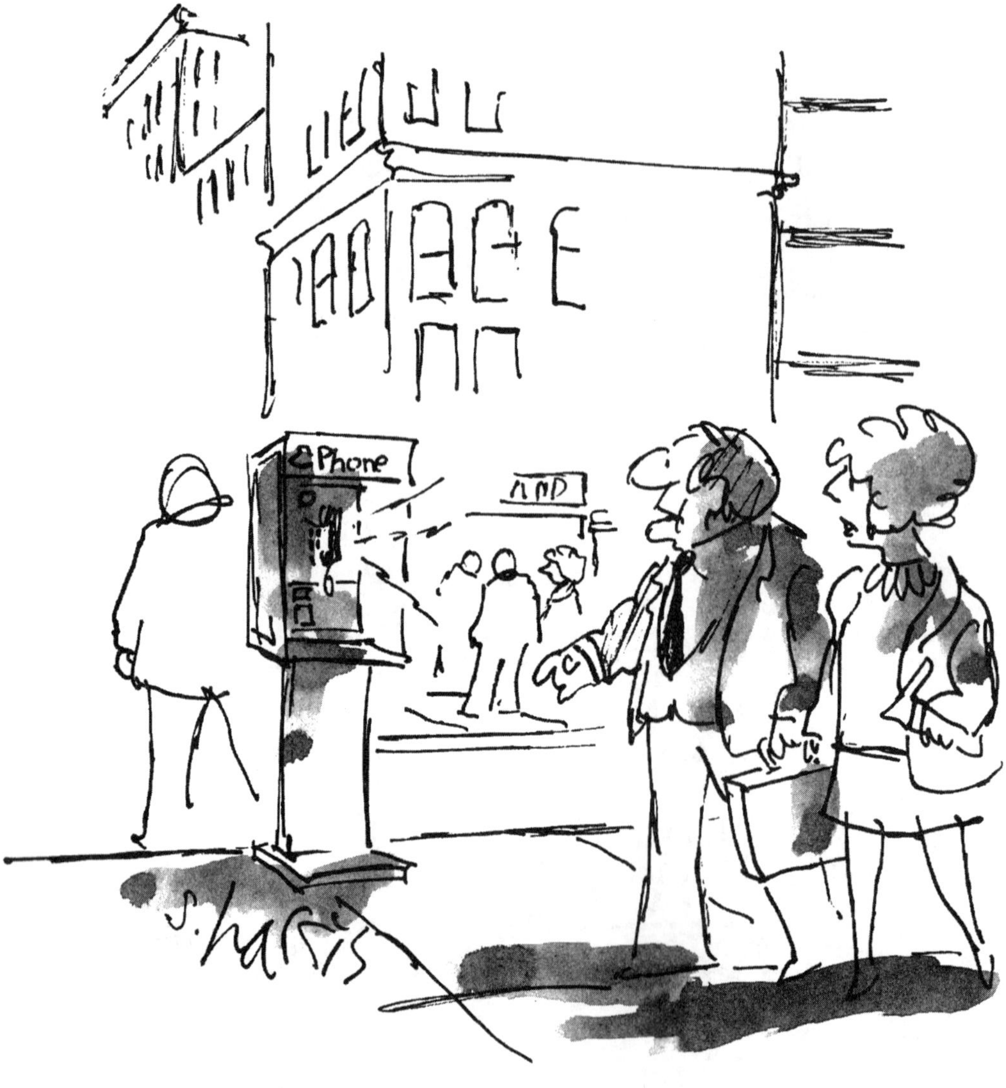

Phone
S. Harris

"That's for me. I have call forwarding."

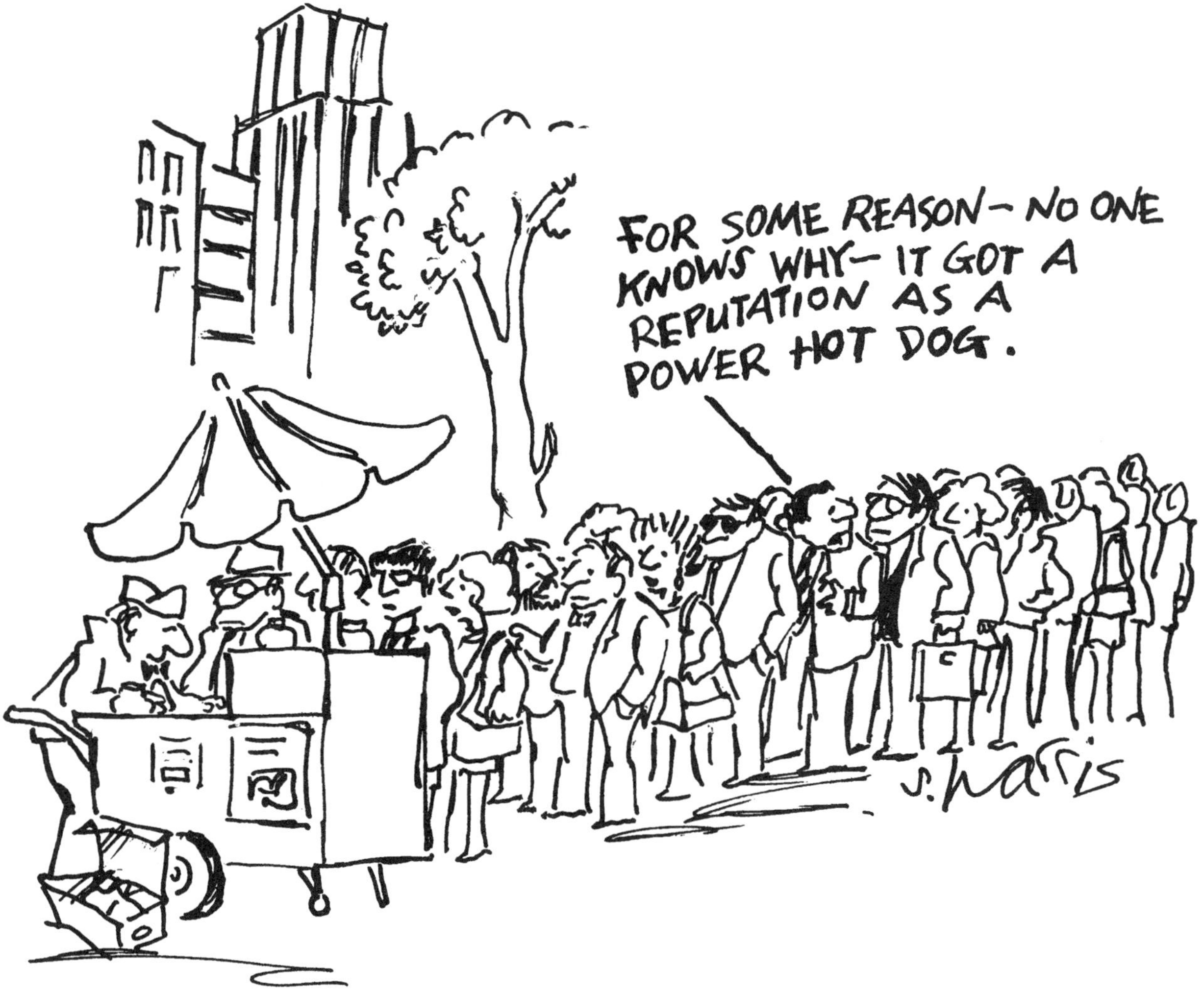
FOR SOME REASON— NO ONE KNOWS WHY— IT GOT A REPUTATION AS A POWER HOT DOG.
S. Harris

"*Just take a look at this on-board computer. It can figure square roots, percentages and the interest rate of your monthly installment.*"

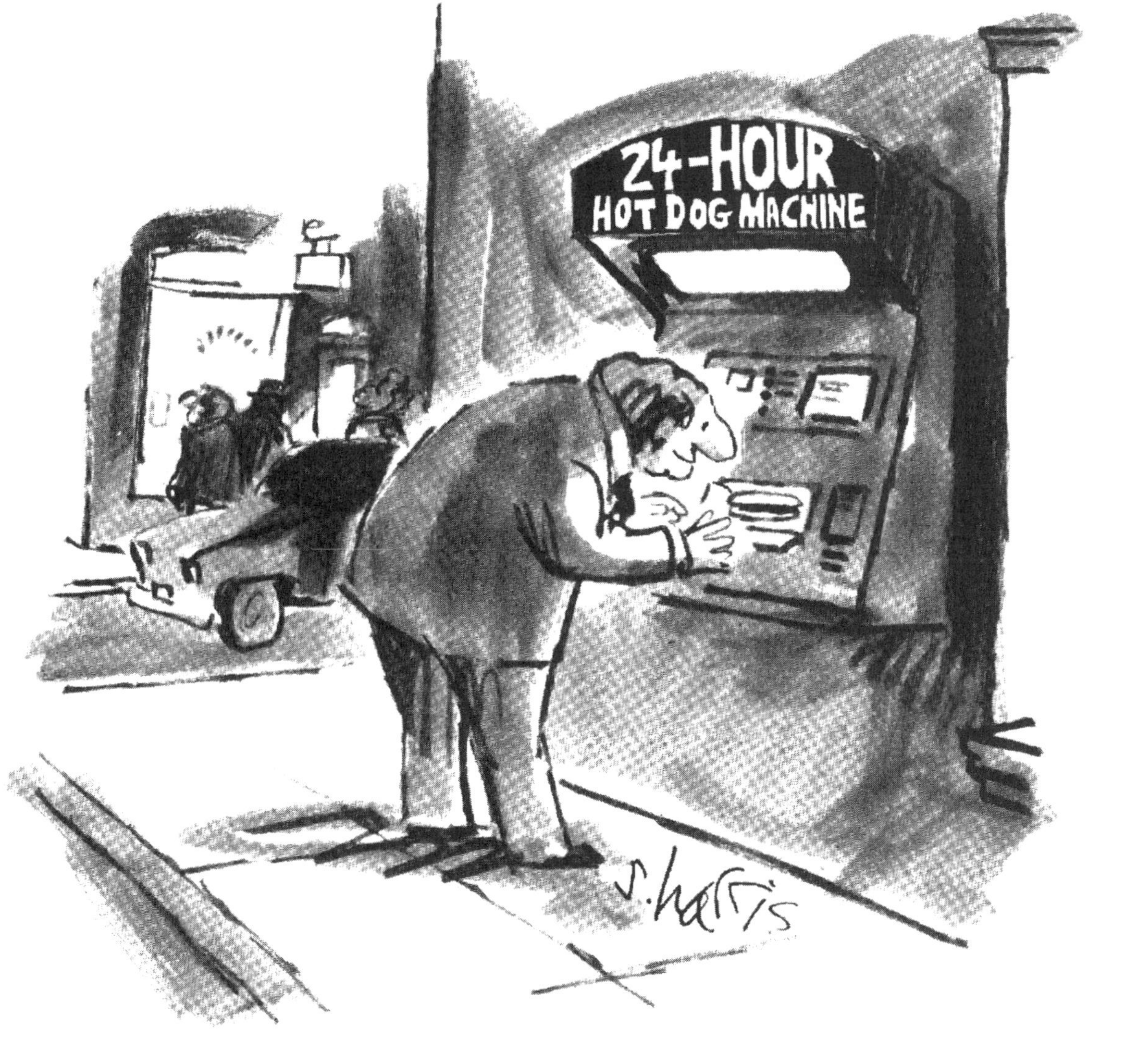
24-HOUR
HOT DOG MACHINE
S. Harris

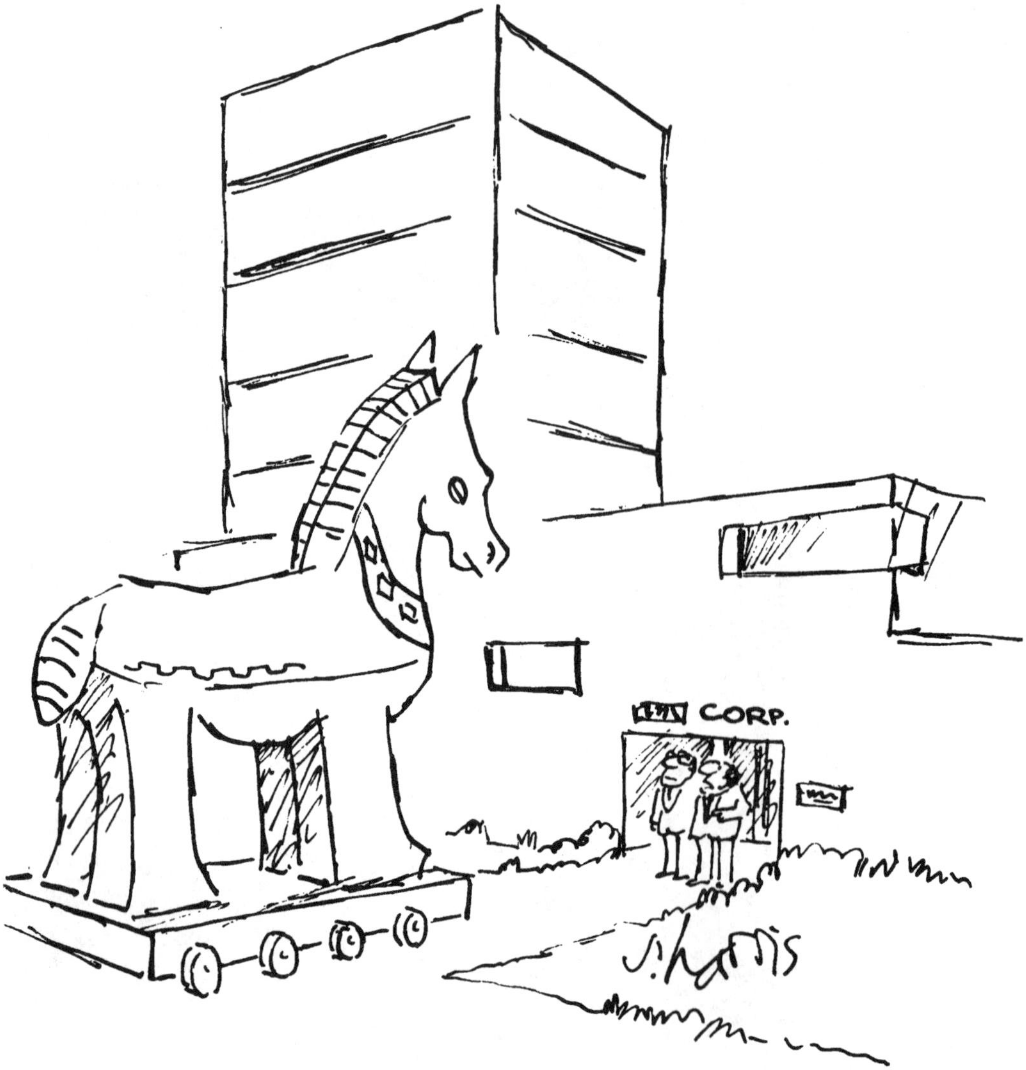
CORP.
S. Harris

"I'd say it's some sort of take over attempt."

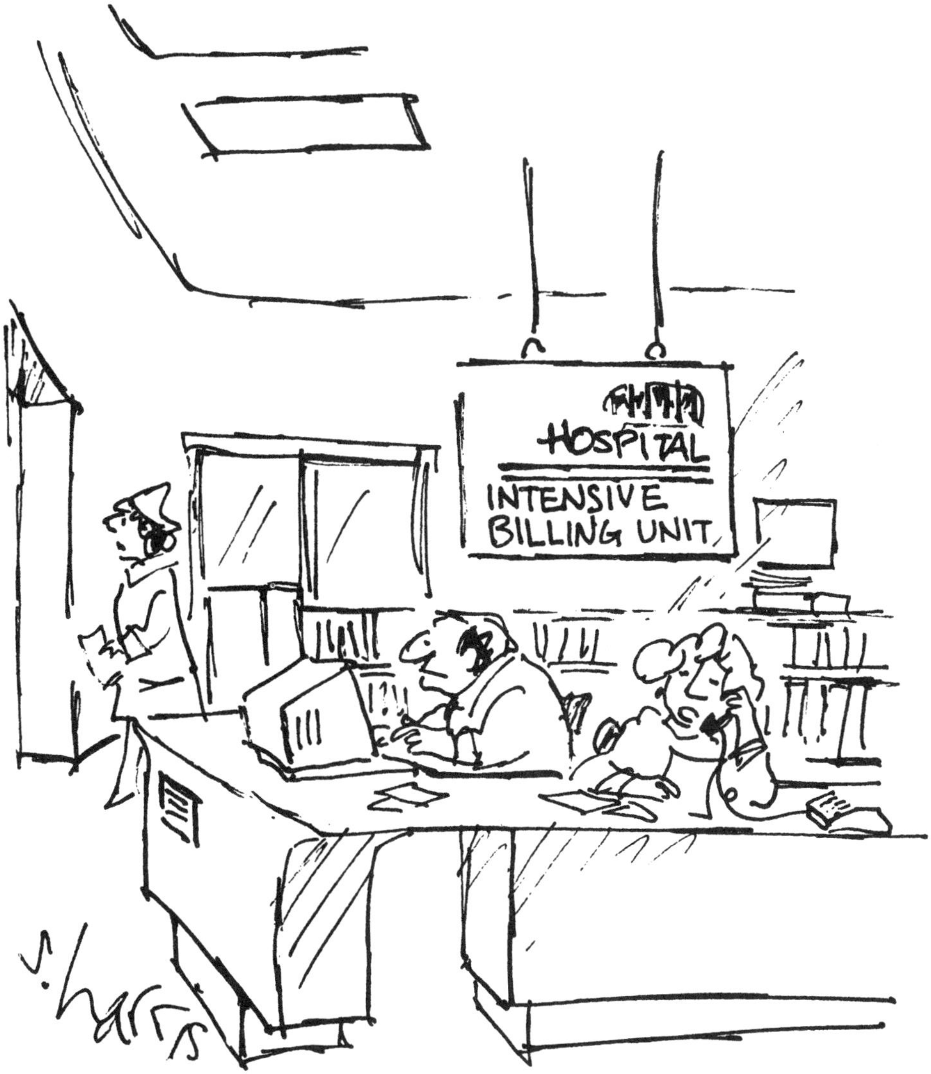
HOSPITAL
INTENSIVE
BILLING UNIT
S. Harris

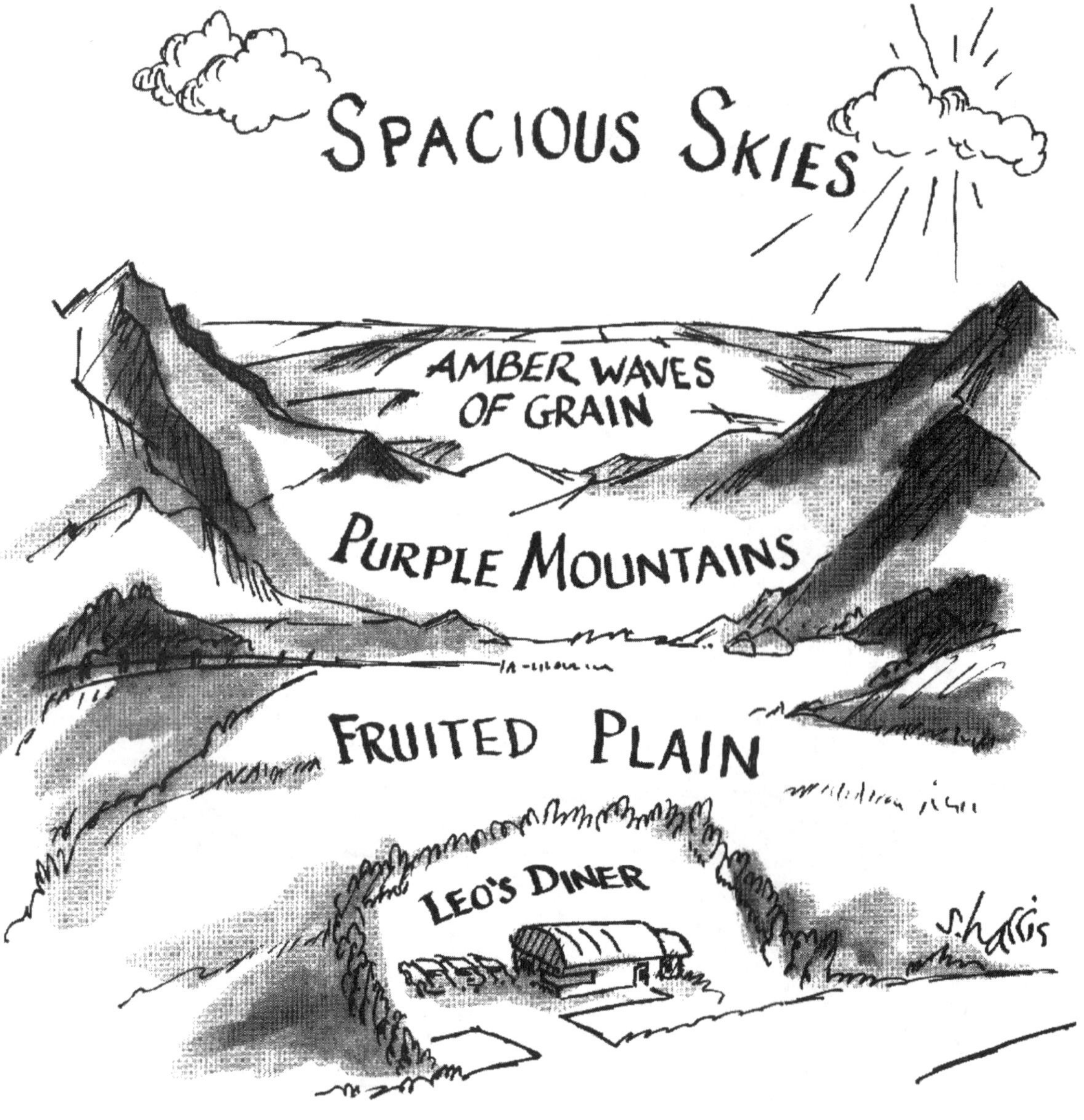
SPACIOUS SKIES
AMBER WAVES OF GRAIN
PURPLE MOUNTAINS
FRUITED PLAIN
LEO'S DINER
s.harris